Understanding Bible Prophecy

Understanding Bible Prophecy

or
God's Plan for the Future

Presented by
Edmund Berkeley Hammond

iUniverse, Inc.
Bloomington

Understanding Bible Prophecy
God's Plan for the Future

iUniverse books may be ordered through booksellers or by contacting:

iUniverse
1663 Liberty Drive
Bloomington, IN 47403
www.iuniverse.com
1-800-Authors (1-800-288-4677)

ISBN: 978-1-4620-2120-8 (sc)
ISBN: 978-1-4620-1947-2 (e)

Printed in the United States of America

iUniverse rev. date: 07/18/2011

PREFACE

Of the 66 books of the Bible, 18 are devoted entirely to prophecy, showing that God considers the prophetic scriptures to be quite important. However, the messages that these prophetic books contain are often difficult to comprehend. It is the purpose of this book to provide its readers with a better understanding of these prophetic messages, especially those that relate to end-time events, i.e., eschatological events.

These somewhat complex messages were given to the writers by the Holy Spirit of God, and He is the only One qualified to interpret them correctly. In John 16:13 Jesus stated that the Holy Spirit will lead us into all truth, giving us His words of wisdom and knowledge as necessary. Without His assistance in recognizing prophetic truth, the teachings presented in this book will be just another set of human opinions.

The first article that is presented in this book introduces the reader to the Revelation to John, which is considered to be the "backbone" of eschatology. A complete understanding of the format, structure and purpose of the Revelation is definitely required if God's plans for the future are to be fully understood.

I pray that the Holy Spirit will highlight any truths that are contained in the teachings of this book and help those who read it to better comprehend God's prophetic messages, especially those relating to the events that are about to take place on this earth.

ACKNOWLEDGEMENTS

I am deeply indebted to God for sending His Holy Spirit to help me interpret and understand the prophecies of the Bible, and for assisting me in writing this document. Without His encouragement and assistance this book could never have been written.

I also wish to extend my sincere thanks to my son, John Elwyn, for the many hours that he spent in editing the manuscript for this book. His editing experience was a real asset in preparing this book for publication.

In conclusion, let me thank all of my devoted friends and associates who encouraged me to publish several of my short articles in book form. Without their prompting, this publication project probably would never have been initiated.

E. "Berk" Hammond

UNDERSTANDING BIBLE PROPHECY
By: Edmund Berkeley Hammond
(First released in April 2011)

*   *   *   *   *   *   *

TABLE OF CONTENTS

INTRODUCTION
My Personal Testimony

My introduction to the power of the Holy Spirit came in October, 1972, when I was baptized with the Holy Spirit. Although that was a memorable event in itself, for the sake of brevity I will not describe it here. Suffice to say that I have received and used several of the supernatural spiritual gifts listed in 1 Cor. 12:8-11 in the years following my baptism with the Holy Spirit.

About two weeks after receiving this spiritual baptism, God gave me a special call in an extraordinary manner. Early one morning as I was saying my devotional prayers, I began to pray for my earthly father, who, at the age of 83, was living with my sister in South Carolina. He was in fairly good health, although he had experienced some problems with his heart, and I prayed that when the time would come for him to be taken to his heavenly home, he would be granted an easy passing, without an extended period of suffering.

While I was praying in this manner, I received a vision from God. I saw before me a single page of a calendar with one of the days on it circled in red; the date was Thursday, May 3, 1973, about seven months in the future. The vision was similar in many respects to a hologram, with which most scientists should be familiar. This was the first and only vision that I have ever received from God, and I was quite surprised and somewhat confused by it.

I asked God about the meaning of this vision. He told me that the date circled on the calendar had been tentatively selected for my father's physical death. Then He said that He had two primary reasons for giving me this advanced knowledge:

1. He knew that my work schedule would be quite heavy at the time of my father's death, and I was told to schedule a week of vacation at about that time in order to be away from the pressure of office work at the time of his funeral.

2. He was calling me to be an interpreter of some of the more controversial scriptures in the Bible, especially the eschatological passages that He considered to be quite important. He indicated His displeasure with the way in which so many different interpretations of these critical passages of scripture have arisen within His church body, working to destroy the unity that He desires to see within His church.

Then God reminded me of two Bible verses (Deut. 18:21-22), which essentially state that a true prophet can be identified by the accuracy of his predictions. When He gave me this vision He took on the role of a prophet, predicting the approximate time of my father's death. Consequently, if and when his death did occur as predicted, I could know that this message came from God and not from some other source.

One might expect that based on this information, I would hasten to make my father's salvation certain, so that he would be ready to go at the predicted time of his departure. However, this was not necessary, for he had been a devout Christian all of his life. As an example of his dedication, he had been the Superintendent of a Baptist Sunday School for 38 years. So, after discussing the vision with my wife, we decided that it would be best for my father not to know about the message that I had been given, and so we kept it to ourselves.

In accordance with God's instructions I tried to plan a vacation for the specified week in May. For several reasons, this vacation absence could not be arranged for the week including May 3, but because the Lord had said that this date was tentative, the preceding week was scheduled instead. His prediction was not that my father would die on May 3, but that he would die while I was away from my office at a time near May 3.

My wife and I decided to spend this vacation week with my former supervisor who had retired in Florida. We did not believe that there was anything we could do for my father at the time of his death, and furthermore it would be quite easy to return from Florida to South Carolina for his funeral service when that became necessary. I discovered later that God had a special reason for leading us to make that decision.

My ex-supervisor was an agnostic, and he needed to hear my testimony relating to my supernatural call from God. In fact, it became the primary means for leading him to become a charismatic Christian at a later time.

We had been in Florida for only one day when the news of my father's death came to us via a telephone call from my sister. My father had complained of some chest pains early that morning and later, when they became worse, an ambulance was called. However, he died of a heart attack en route to the hospital. Thus my prayer request for a quick and relatively painless death for my father had been answered, and the divine source of my vision was confirmed.

The immediate result of my call from God was a new and intense desire to read the Bible, especially the prophetic scriptures. Whenever I found it necessary to take a business trip, I would always take my Bible with me and read it at every opportunity. This practice continued for about twelve years, and then God finally instructed me to begin writing some short papers on controversial subjects that He would select for me.

As these papers were completed, I was led to send copies to those persons who might benefit from reading them. To date, I have written more than 20 such documents, and I have distributed over a thousand printed copies to my friends and to others to whom the Holy Spirit directed me.

Please be advised that the primary spiritual gift that I received from God was not the gift of prophecy, as one might suppose, although on a few special occasions I have received and used this gift. Instead, God has used the word of knowledge and the word of wisdom quite frequently to show me the way in which certain scripture passages can be used to interpret other passages. He has given me the two following guidelines for my use in interpreting scripture passages:

1. In accordance with 2 Tim. 3:16-17, "*all scripture is inspired by God and profitable for teaching, for reproof, for correction, for training in righteousness; that the man of God may be*

adequate, equipped for every good work." This means that all scripture is infallible.

2. God also reminded me on several occasions that He never contradicts Himself, therefore in order to be valid, any interpretation or explanation of scripture must satisfy every Biblical passage that relates to the topic under consideration.

Each of the articles that I have written has been based on these two principles, and any person who does not accept and embrace these standards of interpretation is not likely to be satisfied with the conclusions that I have reached.

Considering the experiences to which I have been exposed, some of my friends and acquaintances tend to regard me as a "modern prophet," and to the extent that I have been led by God to proclaim certain segments of His truth to the public, this prophetic label might be somewhat appropriate. However, the call that God has given me differs from the call given to the Biblical prophets in that their calls were usually to present God's messages to certain specified recipients for the first time, whereas I have been called to provide a proper interpretation for previous prophetic messages contained in the Bible. Therefore, it is apparent that I was called to be a Bible teacher rather than a prophet.

Concluding Remarks

Several of my friends requested me to incorporate my papers into one or more books, and I agreed to do this. This book is my first attempt to publish my papers in book form, and it includes a selection of my papers that relate to eschatological events. These documents are not listed in the order in which they were first written; instead, they are presented in the order that makes them easier to read and understand.

All of the papers presented herein were written as independent documents dealing with specific eschatological topics; consequently, some topics may be covered in more than one document. However, every effort has been made to hold the number of these redundant texts to a minimum.

I pray that the Holy Spirit will guide all those who read this book and help them to understand the interpretations that are presented herein. Any credit for these articles must go to God Himself, for if He had not given me my supernatural call and then coached me for many years in the interpretation of His prophetic scriptures, these documents would not exist today.

I thank God for His call and for His continued presence in my life, and I look forward to meeting with Jesus and my many Christian friends when He comes to gather us unto Himself.

E. "Berk" Hammond

* * * * * * *

A BRIEF DESCRIPTION OF THE INCLUDED DOCUMENTS

This book is the primary source of information for the study of eschatological topics, and its purpose and format are explored here.

This article provides a scenario of the major end-time events, showing their interrelationship. This teaching is based primarily on the testimony of Jesus, since in Rev. 19:10 we are told that "...the testimony of Jesus is the spirit of prophecy."

The Book of Leviticus describes seven feasts that the Jews are required to celebrate each year. However, Deut. 16:16 and 2 Chron. 8:13 both indicate that God has identified three of these feasts as being of special importance to Him – the Feast of Unleavened Bread, the Feast of Weeks, and the Feast of Tabernacles. This article examines the spiritual significance of these three feasts.

This article provides an in-depth study of the meaning and the implications of Jesus' parable of the Tares in the Wheat Field.

The non-Christian Jews are now living under their old covenant that was originally given to Abraham. This article explores what the Bible has to say about their eventual destiny.

* * * * * * *

NOTE: The twelve articles listed above provide interpretations for selected prophetic passages of the Bible, therefore, its readers should have a copy of the Bible handy for reference purposes. All Bible quotations that are recorded in these documents are taken from the New King James Version of the Bible unless otherwise specified.

AN INTRODUCTION TO THE REVELATION TO JOHN
(First released in February 1985)

*   *   *   *   *   *   *

Contents

F.   Section 2—The Main Apocalyptic Message—Chapters 8–22

  1.   Seven Trumpets, Heralding Christ's Return to Earth

  2.   Two Major Events Following the Seventh Trumpet

  3.   The Millennium

  4.   The Post-Millennial Period

G.   Summary and Conclusions

*   *   *   *   *   *   *

Preliminary Remarks

Theologians have interpreted the Revelation to St. John the Divine in many different ways. Some consider it to be a message that was written primarily to provide encouragement for the Christians who were under persecution near the end of the First Century. Others believe that it contains a hidden message that is directed to, and can be understood only by, those who live near the close of the church age. Still another group emphasizes the fact that it seems to have been written in the literary form of a Greek drama so as to be presented on a stage. Obviously, all of these interpretations cannot be entirely correct, although there might be an element of truth in each of them.

It seems that most of the interpretive books that have been written concerning the Revelation to John contain some truth, based upon specific revelations given to the individual authors by the Holy Spirit. However, if and when they attempt to expand their specific revelations into an interpretation of the entire book, these authors have in many cases considered it necessary to rely on their own imaginations and interpretive logic, leading to widely differing conclusions.

It is not the purpose of this brief document to provide still another interpretation of the Revelation to John. Instead, its purpose is to present some pertinent ideas concerning the format, structure and purpose of the book as the Holy Spirit has revealed them. Of course, in writing a document of this type, it is impossible to avoid inserting a few interpretations in order to reach a better understanding of the contents of the book, but they will be held to a minimum. This document might be considered to be a "road map" into the Revelation of St. John the Divine.

Three basic categories of questions can be raised concerning the Revelation to John as follows:

1. Is the particular text under consideration to be interpreted literally or figuratively?

2. If figuratively, what is its symbolic code?

3. What was God's primary reason for including the passage in the book?

This document will be devoted primarily to questions of the third type, assuming that the Holy Spirit will provide readers with answers to questions of the first two types as they occur.

It is my opinion that any person who has not received the baptism with the Holy Spirit is not likely to receive much from reading the Revelation to John. God and Christ Jesus were the real authors of this book, using the Holy Spirit to transfer their words to St. John the Divine. Because the Holy Spirit is the Divine Being who gave the words for John to write, He is the only one qualified to interpret them for the reader, using His gift of the word of knowledge. Remember that Jesus promised us: *"However, when He, the Spirit of truth, has come, He will guide you into all truth; for He will not speak on His own authority, but whatever He hears He will speak; and He will tell you things to come." (John 16:13).* We should always ask Him to guide our thoughts as we study the Revelation to John.

It is my hope that this document will provide assistance to anyone who desires to study the Revelation by clarifying its format and by identifying the most important things to consider while reading it. A document such as this would have been quite helpful to me during my first attempts to read and understand this mysterious piece of apocalyptic literature.

The Name of the Book

The first thing to be realized is that the book has a somewhat misleading name. In some Bible translations, it has been called the "Revelation of St. John," which might lead one to believe that St. John was its author. However, this erroneous assumption is clarified in Verses 1 and 2 of Chapter 1:

> *(1) The Revelation of Jesus Christ, which God gave Him to show His servants - things which must shortly take place. And He sent and signified it by His angel to His servant John,*
> *(2) who bore witness to the word of God and to the testimony of Jesus Christ, to all things that he saw.*

From these verses it is evident that the true author of the book is God the Father, who revealed its contents to His Son, Christ Jesus, who in turn revealed them to His servant John through His angel. John's only function was to write down the words that were given to him and to describe his visions without any changes or modifications (see Rev. 22:18-19). Therefore it is not necessary that we know anything about St. John's background or his understanding of prior prophetic literature; we only need to know that he was a competent and trustworthy stenographer. He may or may not have been John the Apostle, but his identification is not a prerequisite for understanding the prophetic messages contained in the book.

The Primary Purpose of the Book

At this point it might be well to consider the real purpose of the book, and with the help of the Holy Spirit, to obtain an overall view of its prophetic message. After all, there are many prophetic books in the Old Testament that contain apocalyptic passages, so why did God decide that another prophetic book was required for the New Testament?

In considering this question it will be helpful to list some of the ways in which the Revelation to John is unique. A few specific examples of its uniqueness are:

1. It is the only entirely prophetic book of the Bible that was written in the form of a letter.

2. It is the only book for which God and Christ Jesus are the expressed authors, and which contains a specific warning against making any changes to its contents.

3. It was given to the transcriber (St. John) by means of a series of messages or visions, and many of the predicted events were witnessed spiritually by John. Earlier prophets

declared the words of God, and some occasionally received spectacular visions; but it is unlikely that any of them ever received their series of messages at one time, as did St. John the Divine.

4. It is the last prophetic book to be written and included as a part of the Biblical canon.

5. It is the only book of the Bible, devoted entirely to prophecy, that was written during the church age, i.e., subsequent to Pentecost.

6. It is the only prophetic book to be addressed primarily to the Christian church, rather than to the nation Israel.

7. It is the only prophetic book that emphasizes the sequence and order of the predicted events, e.g., seven consecutive seals of the scroll, seven consecutive trumpet blasts, and seven consecutive bowls of God's wrath.

From this list it is obvious that the Revelation to John is a very special and unique book and that it deserves special attention and careful study by all Christians.

In searching for the primary purpose for this divinely inspired letter, it seems that the seventh example of its uniqueness listed above affords the best clue. As was stated before, the prophetic books of the Old Testament do contain many apocalyptic passages. However, those passages for the most part are intermingled with others relating to the first coming of Christ Jesus or to contemporary prophecy in such a way that placing them in their proper sequential order can be quite difficult.

This was one of the major problems confronting the Jews at the time of Jesus' first visit to earth. They had read the apocalyptic prophecies concerning the Second Coming of their Messiah as a conquering King (e.g., Zech. 14) but, either intentionally or unintentionally, they overlooked passages describing His first mission as the sacrificial Lamb of God (see Isaiah 53).

It has been shown that the Revelation to John highlights the sequence and order of events at the close of the church age. Therefore we may conclude that its primary purpose is: (1) to disclose God's plan for redeeming the world from Satan, and (2) to show the members of the Christian church the way in which all prior eschatological prophecies must be merged together in time sequence to create the scenario of events to be expected at the close of the church age.

The Structure of the Book

The Revelation to John describes the major events to be expected at the close of the church age; that is, it is an eschatological book. The book is divided into only two major sections – (1) the introduction, and (2) the main apocalyptic message. The first seven chapters of the book are introductory chapters, and the last fifteen chapters present the apocalyptic message.

One mistake individuals frequently make in trying to interpret the Revelation to John is to consider some scripture passage in the introductory section of the book as a part of the main apocalyptic message. However, this leads to an erroneous concept of the timing of that eschatological event. The first seven chapters are introductory chapters, leading to the main apocalyptic message beginning in Chapter 8. If the timing of a specific event in or following the tribulation period is to be understood, that event must be found in Chapters 8-22, which disclose the main apocalyptic events in chronological order.

SECTION I – The Introductory Section

It should be recognized that this book is written in the form of a letter, and its format is similar to that of the Pauline Epistles. The contents of the first seven introductory chapters of this letter can be outlined briefly as follows.

The Divine Introduction – Chapter I

This chapter begins by introducing the authors of the book (God the Father and Christ Jesus), the transcriber (St. John the Divine) and the seven specific churches in Asia Minor that were designated to be the recipients of the letter. This chapter also includes a rather elaborate salutation or greeting.

The Seven Recipient Churches – Chapters 2-3

Because Jesus gave the main apocalyptic message to John for the benefit of a church group that would exist many centuries later, it was necessary to provide a way to preserve the message for this long length of time. This was accomplished by selecting seven churches in Asia Minor to be the recipients of the letter. Since the number seven is usually used in prophetic literature to indicate completeness, then it may be concluded that the letter was really addressed to the entire Christian church. It was to be held in safekeeping by these seven churches, and later by successive churches, until the church age finally comes to an end. The message was directed primarily to the church body that will be in existence at the end of the church age; they are the only group that will be able to fully comprehend its meaning.

There was another obstacle to the preservation of the letter that required God's special attention – the seven churches had to be convinced of the validity of the message contained in the letter. After all, the church leaders only had John's word concerning the way in which he had received the letter, and more proof of its validity was required in order to justify recording and distributing it to other Christian churches, to say nothing of believing its message themselves.

Jesus convinced them that the message really came from Him by including in the text of each letter a short personalized message to the church being addressed, a message that contained intimate details relating to its members that could be known only by God and Christ Jesus. By this means they were convinced that the messages were valid and that they could not be ignored.

Some church historians have suggested that one or more of these seven churches may not have been in existence at the time that the Revelation was given to John. Should this be true, then such a prophetic prediction of the strengths and weaknesses of any church prior to its formation would provide additional proof that the authors of the letter were in fact God and Christ Jesus. Such foreknowledge would have to come from them alone.

There are also some who believe that each of the seven recipient churches is symbolic of a definite and sequential time period in the life of the entire Christian church, beginning with the church in Ephesus and ending with the church in Laodicea. This view is supported to some degree by the prediction Paul gave in 2 Thess. 2:1-4, stating that a "falling away" (an apostasy) would occur within the church before the Christians are taken to be with Christ. This "falling away" seems to be exemplified by the lukewarm condition of the Laodicean church.

Although it is evident that the Christian church body today does exhibit to a certain degree the lukewarm attitude that was ascribed to the church in Laodicea, it also resembles the other six churches to some extent. For example, many in the church today appear to have lost their first love for God and for Christ Jesus, as did the members of the Ephesian church. Also, many of our churches are encountering the problem of sexual promiscuity being practiced by their members, as did the church in Pergamum; and many of our works-oriented churches have active programs but are dead spiritually, as was the church in Sardis. Therefore since the specific sins attributed to each of the seven recipient churches can be found to some extent in many of our churches today, all Christians should heed and follow the advice given to each of these seven churches.

Recognize that the main apocalyptic message given in Section 2 predicts a series of prophetic events that will take place at or near the close of the church age, therefore the seven recipient churches could not expect to see them fulfilled within their lifetimes. This prophetic message was probably too difficult for them to understand, and they were certain to be tempted to alter the text somewhat in order to make it more meaningful to the Christians of their time.

However, Jesus warned them against taking such action in Rev. 22:18-19 by saying:

> (18) *I testify to everyone who hears the words of the prophecy of this book: If anyone adds to these things, God will add to him the plagues that are written in this book;*
> (19) *and if anyone takes away from the words of the book of this prophecy, God shall take away his part from the Book of Life, from the holy city, and from the things which are written in this book.*

From this quotation it is apparent that: (1) Jesus considered the message of the letter to be of great value to the entire church, and (2) those who would receive it first would probably not understand it and would be tempted to edit its contents.

John's Visit to God's Throne Room – Chapters 4-5

Chapters 4 and 5 describe John's visit to God's throne room in heaven. This was John's formal introduction to the two authors of the book – God the Father and Christ Jesus, His Son. Chapter 4 provides a description of God's throne room, with all of His attendant spiritual beings. Chapter 5 introduces the Lamb of God, Christ Jesus. The twenty-four elders around God's throne are considered to be the heads of the twelve tribes of Israel and Jesus' twelve apostles. It is significant to note that when the holy city, the New Jerusalem, eventually comes to rest on the new earth, its twelve gates will bear the names of the twelve tribes of Israel, and its twelve foundations will be named for the twelve apostles of Jesus (see Rev. 21:12-14).

It is also interesting to note that John does not give a good description of God the Father – he simply refers to Him as *"One who sat on the throne."* This leads to the conclusion that John did not actually see all of God the Father. According to Exodus 33:20 God once told Moses: *"You cannot see My face; for no man shall see Me and live."* Likewise, in Chapter 5, Christ Jesus is not described as a man, but rather as the "Lamb of God."

The Lamb of God and the Sealed Scroll – Chapter 5

In Rev. 5:1, John is shown a scroll in the hand of the *"One who sat on the throne,"* and the scroll was sealed with seven seals. Verses 2-4 describe an unsuccessful angelic search for someone having the authority to break the seals and open the scroll. But this search ends in Verse 5 when one of the elders around God's throne tells John: *"Do not weep. Behold, the Lion of the tribe of Judah, the Root of David, has prevailed to open the scroll and to loose its seven seals."*

At the time of creation, God gave Adam and Eve dominion over the entire earth and its contents (see Genesis 1:27-30), but because of their subsequent transgressions under the influence of Satan, their title to the earth was lost to Satan. The scroll described in Rev. 5 will be found to present the various stages in God's overall plan to redeem the world from Satan, beginning with the release of the spirit of the Antichrist in Rev. 6:2 and ending with the initiation of the final seven-year tribulation period in Rev. 8:1.

Throughout this future seven-year period of tribulation, each year will begin with the sounding of an angelic trumpet. And when the last trumpet has been sounded, God will finally take command of the kingdoms of the world.

The text of Rev. 11:15 confirms this transfer of power and authority from Satan to God: "*Then the seventh angel sounded: And there were loud voices in heaven, saying, 'The kingdoms of this world have become the kingdoms of our Lord and of His Christ, and He shall reign forever and ever!'*"

The seven seals that bind the scroll describe briefly and symbolically the different phases of God's plan for reclaiming the world from Satan. The messages covered by these seals are listed in Rev. 6:1 through 8:1 – they describe the rather drastic conditions that God will impose on the citizens of the world prior to the Second Coming of Christ Jesus.

Only those Christians who remain faithful to God and to Jesus throughout the time of their exposure to these severe conditions will be taken into heaven via the harvest rapture, described in Rev. 14:14-16. Likewise, only those non-Christians who continue to live righteous lives during this time period will be allowed to remain as inhabitants of the redeemed earth. Remember that in Matt. 24:13, Jesus stated: "*But he who endures to the end shall be saved.*"

This divine plan of God can be divided into several segments, which are described briefly in the text that follows.

The Messages on the Scroll – Chapter 6

The breaking of the first four seals release four horsemen that are often referred to as the "four horsemen of the apocalypse." Their colored horses are similar in many respects to those drawing the four chariots described in Zech. 6:1-8, which an angel described as the "four spirits of heaven." It is therefore quite likely that the four horsemen of Rev. 6 also represent four spirits of heaven (the spirits of the Antichrist, war and anarchy, famine, and death) and that they were all released simultaneously in the first century A.D.

Apparently the mission of these tormenting spirits is to provide the citizens of God's kingdom opportunities to exercise and strengthen their faith, for it has been found that our faith grows only in times of persecution. Our Christian faith is very important to God, for we are told in Heb. 11:6 that without faith it is impossible to please Him, and persecution is the "fertilizer" that causes a Christian's faith to grow strong.

When the fifth seal was broken, John saw the souls of the Christian martyrs resting together under the altar of God in Paradise, asking that their blood be avenged by judging those who had caused their deaths. However, they were told to wait until those who were still alive on earth and destined to be martyrs had been killed. This passage indicates that throughout the entire church age Christians will be killed because of their faith in Christ Jesus.

God's reason for giving special recognition to the Christian martyrs is not entirely obvious. After all, the spirit of death was released following the breaking of the fourth seal, so why would it be necessary to highlight the group that had died as martyrs? The answer to this question seems to relate to the place in which the souls of these martyrs are residing – under the divine altar in paradise.

It is before this altar that the future marriage ceremony – bonding Christ Jesus to His church bride – is likely to be held. Therefore, it seems reasonable to conclude that the Christian martyrs will constitute the true bride of Christ. They are fully qualified to hold this position because they have given their lives for Jesus, just as He gave His life for them on the cross. They are shown to be waiting under the altar, presumably anticipating the beginning of the marriage ceremony.

Other Christians will constitute the body of Christ, but after the marriage ceremony has been concluded these two groups will "become one flesh" and will become indistinguishable from each other. It seems obvious that God's purpose in highlighting these Christian martyrs is to show His intention to provide a fully qualified bride for His Son, Christ Jesus.

From the wording of Rev. 6:12-17 it is clear that the breaking of the sixth seal brings a preview of a series of cataclysmic events that will be experienced during the outpouring of God's wrath, described later in Chapter 16. In fact, Rev. 6:17 contains the statement: *"For the great day of His wrath has come, and who is able to stand?"* Therefore, it is quite evident that God plans to impose a period of very intense tribulation and suffering on all non-Christians as a part of His program for redeeming the world from Satan. A comparison of the events described in Rev. 6:12-17 with those listed in Rev. 16 will disclose many similarities. When God displays His wrath, He will remove all evildoers and troublemakers from the earth in order to keep them from interfering with the rulers and citizens of Christ's millennial kingdom.

Immediately following the outpouring of God's wrath, Jesus will return and judge the remaining inhabitants of the earth in the "judgment of the nations." This judgment is described in Matt. 25:31-46, and it will be noted that the "goats" (the remaining non-Christian evildoers and troublemakers) will be cast into the lake of fire (see Verse 41). This will complete the cleanup of the earth prior to the start of Christ's 1,000-year reign on the earth.

God's Two Servant Groups – Chapter 7

Chapter 7 of the Revelation to John contains two special messages constituting a preview of two important events that will take place during the tribulation period. These are: (1) the selection of the 144,000 Jewish bondservants of Christ, and (2) the transfer of the Christian saints from earth into heaven via the final harvest rapture. Note, however, that because this chapter is not a part of the main apocalyptic message starting in Chapter 8, the details given here do not contribute any information concerning the timing of these two events.

The first eight verses of this chapter are devoted to a description of the way in which the 144,000 Jewish bondservants will be chosen – 12,000 from each of twelve tribes of Israel. Then from Rev. 14:4 it is apparent that all of these bondservants will be celibate men, given to Christ Jesus by God the Father, probably as a wedding present to celebrate His marriage to the saints of the Christian church.

The remainder of Chapter 7 is devoted to a description of the way in which the souls of the Christian saints will be treated after their arrival in paradise following the harvest rapture. In another of my documents titled "Closing Events of the Church Age," I explain that there will be two different types of Christians to be taken in the harvest rapture – (1) those who have been chosen to be rulers under Christ Jesus during the Millennium and thereafter, and (2) those who have been called to be servants of God in His heavenly temple (see Rev. 7:15).

Remember that according to 2 Cor. 5:10, "*...we must all appear before the judgment seat of Christ, so that each one may receive what is due for what he has done in the body, whether good or evil.*" (ESV) Therefore it is quite likely that the first event that all of these raptured Christians will experience will be the judgment of their works by Christ Jesus. This subject is discussed in more detail in another of my articles titled "God's Four Proclaimed Judgments."

The Breaking of the Seventh Seal – Chapter 8:1

The seventh seal introduces the final seven-year period of tribulation, which will end with the outpouring of God's wrath. According to Rev. 3:10 the purpose of this tribulation period will be to test the faith of all those living on the earth. The specific events of this tribulation period are outlined in Chapters 8-19.

The first verse of Chapter 8 tells of a short period of complete silence in heaven immediately following the breaking of this last seal. This verse reads as follows: *"When He opened the seventh seal, there was silence in heaven for about half an hour."* This short period of silence will come over the citizens of heaven when they contemplate the intense suffering and the disasters that will be brought on the citizens of earth during the next seven years.

Jesus described this time of suffering in Matt. 24: 21-22 using these words: *"For then there will be great tribulation, such as has not been since the beginning of the world until this time, no, nor ever shall be. And unless those days were shortened, no flesh would be saved; but for the elect's sake those days will be shortened."* This passage shows the real reason for silence in heaven when the tribulation period is announced by the breaking of the seventh seal.

SECTION 2 – The Main Apocalyptic Message

For anyone who may have read the Revelation to John but a few times, it may be difficult to see how the book presents a schedule for end-time events in an orderly manner. In order to understand the main apocalyptic message that begins in Chapter 8, it is necessary to recognize and distinguish between two basically different types of passages that are found in this section.

First, there are the passages that contain the predicted events in their proper time sequence, and the remaining chapters or verses can be defined as "interlude passages." These interludes can be considered to be enlarged footnotes used either to amplify the message at a particular point or to introduce another series of events that will take place at approximately the same time. Once the interlude passages have been identified, then the remaining passages of the main apocalyptic section will disclose the proper sequence of events.

The interlude passages in the Revelation to John are understood to be as follows:

Passage	Interlude Content
Chapter 10	Chapter 10 tells of an angel who gave John some private information that he was not allowed to write into the book, and then he commissioned John to fulfill the role of a prophet. The part of this message that is of primary concern to the church is found in Verses 5-7. Here the angel announces that the sounding of the seventh trumpet will initiate the final episode in God's program for redeeming the world from Satan – the outpouring of His wrath.
Chapter 12	Chapter 12 contains a description of the birth of the 144,000 Hebrew menservants (the "male child" of Verse 5), Satan's expulsion from heaven, and his role as the persecutor of both Israel and the Christian church during the last half of the tribulation period.
Chapter 13	Chapter 13 continues the message of Chapter 12, describing the activities of Satan's two "beasts" during the entire tribulation period. These beasts are: (1) the tyrannical world ruler, often called the Antichrist, and (2) his false prophet.
Chapter 15	Chapter 15 begins by showing a scene in heaven in which the residents of heaven are singing a song of victory. Then the seven angels who will pour out the seven bowls of God's wrath are introduced.
Chapters 17-18	Chapters 17 and 18 provide a detailed description of the judgment and destruction of the harlot "Babylon" in accordance with the angelic proclamation given in Rev. 14:8. This harlot symbolizes a new apostate church – the harlot bride of the Antichrist.

From this it is clear that the main apocalyptic message can be obtained by reading Chapters 8-9, 11, 14, 16, and 19-22 consecutively. One additional thing to remember is that the events described in Chapters 16 and 19 will take place at approximately the same time, since both chapters end with a description of the battle of Armageddon. Chapter 16 describes the events that will take place on earth following the final rapture of the Christian saints, while Chapter 19 describes the series of events that will occur in Paradise at approximately the same time.

The final battle of the tribulation period will be fought at a place called Armageddon (see Rev. 16:16). This battle is described in Rev. 16:17-21 and also in Rev. 19:11-21. Contrary to popular opinion, the battle of Armageddon will not be fought and won using conventional or nuclear weapons; instead, the armies of heaven will use supernatural weapons (thunder, lightning, earthquakes, and 100-pound hailstones) to destroy the armies of the Antichrist.

Please understand that it is not the purpose of this document to provide a detailed verse-by-verse interpretation of the Revelation to John; such a document would be unnecessarily complex and might circumvent the interpretive work of the Holy Spirit for each reader of the book. However, it is considered appropriate to show the major areas into which the main apocalyptic message can be divided and to describe briefly the purpose of each of its segments.

Seven Trumpets, Heralding Christ's Return to Earth

(Chapters 8:2 through 9:21, and Chapter 11)

According to Num. 10:3, 9, trumpets were to be blown by the Israelites for either of two purposes: (1) to assemble the congregation at the meeting tent, or (2) as a warning that the nation is being called to fight in a war. This latter use of trumpets is exemplified in the account of Joshua's attack on Jericho described in Joshua 6:1-21. In this battle God, directed Joshua to have his men of war circle the city, preceded by seven priests blowing seven trumpets, once on each of the six days preceding the day of the attack. Then this procession was to be repeated seven more times on the day of the attack, after which the city would fall to the Israelites.

A pattern similar to this is established in the Revelation to John with the blowing of the seven trumpets preceding the Second Coming of Christ Jesus. It is quite likely that when the angels sound these trumpets, they will be heard supernaturally by all true believers, warning them to be ready to meet their King and to be judged by Him. Remember that in Jesus' parable of the ten virgins the bridesmaids received advance notice of the coming of the bridegroom. It is quite possible that this warning came from their hearing one or more of the tribulational trumpets.

The remainder of the non-Christian world may or may not hear the sounding of these angelic trumpets. In His Olivet Discourse, Jesus predicted that the world at large will be completely surprised by the events at the close of the age, and this may indicate that the trumpets will not be heard by non-Christians. Then in Matt. 24:37-39 Jesus is recorded as saying:

> (37) *But as the days of Noah were, so also will the coming of the Son of Man be.*
> (38) *For as in the days before the flood, they were eating and drinking, marrying and giving in marriage, until the day that Noah entered the ark,*
> (39) *and did not know until the flood came and took them all away, so also shall the coming of the Son of Man be.*

However, there is a passage in the Apocryphal book of 2 Esdras which reads: "*... and the trumpet shall sound aloud, and when all hear it, they shall suddenly be terrified.*" (2 Esdras 6:23 - RSV) The events described in the text following this verse indicate that the trumpet mentioned in this passage is the last (the seventh) trumpet of the tribulation period. It may be that non-Christians will not hear the first six trumpets and will hear only the final trumpet blast, which signals the outpouring of God's wrath and their approaching judgment.

There are many reasons for believing that the period of time covered by the sounding of the seven trumpets in the Revelation to John is identical with the period covered by the Antichrist's seven-year covenant with the nations, described in Dan. 9:27.

Two Major Events Announced
by the Seventh Trumpet

The sounding of the seventh trumpet will initiate two very important events sequentially. These will be: (1) the harvest rapture of the Christian saints, and (2) the outpouring of seven bowls of God's wrath on the inhabitants of the earth.

The sounding of this last trumpet is proclaimed in Rev. 11:15, and the first major action event to follow it will be the harvest rapture of the Christians, described in Rev. 14:14-16. Paul predicted this event in 1 Cor. 15:51-52 when he said the following:

> (51) *Behold, I tell you a mystery: We shall not all sleep,*
> *but we shall all be changed –*
> *(52) in a moment, in the twinkling of an eye, at the last*
> *trumpet. For the trumpet will sound, and the dead will*
> *be raised incorruptible, and we shall be changed.*

After this rapture has occurred the events described in Rev. 16 and 19 will take place. There will be the divine wedding ceremony in heaven, in which Jesus will be permanently bonded to His bride and His church body, and at the same time the seven bowls of God's wrath will be poured out on the citizens of earth. Then Christ Jesus and His army of angels will return to earth to fight the battle of Armageddon.

The outpouring of seven bowls of God's wrath described in Rev. 16 will be the final events of the tribulation period. These events will end with the battle of Armageddon, after which Jesus will return to earth and establish His millennial kingdom. At that time the kingdom of the world will have been finally retrieved from Satan.

The Millennium
(Chapter 20)

The period of 1,000 years during which Christ and His saints will rule over the earth, subdue all of His enemies, and establish peace between all nations without any interference from Satan, is briefly described in Chapter 20. This period ends with the "white throne judgment," in which God will proclaim a final judgment on every soul who has not been resurrected and/or judged previously.

It is apparent from Rev. 20:4-6 that certain selected Christians will be resurrected (i.e., brought back to earth in their spiritual bodies) at the time of Christ's return to earth in order to fulfill their roles as "priests of God and of Christ" and to reign with Him for a thousand years. Then Verse 5 reads as follows: *"But the rest of the dead did not live again until the thousand years were finished. This is the first resurrection."* The "first resurrection" mentioned in this verse is of course the resurrection of the Christians chosen to rule with Christ during the Millennium. This verse also implies that a second resurrection will occur when the "rest of the dead" (the non-Christian dead) are brought to life for their final judgment at the end of the Millennium.

This may be somewhat confusing, since it might seem that the prior resurrection of Christ Jesus would have been called the "first resurrection." However, it appears that in calling this return of the Christian saints to earth a resurrection, a mass resurrection is implied, affecting many people simultaneously. It will be the first resurrection of this type.

The statement given in Rev. 20:6 to the effect that the "second death" will have no power over those included in this first resurrection is quite comforting. Although the individuals who are brought to earth in the first resurrection will be living on earth for a second time, they will have received their imperishable bodies. Therefore they have no need to fear a second physical death when the final white throne judgment takes place and the heavens and the earth are destroyed.

The Post-Millennial Period

(Chapters 21 - 22)

The new heaven (a tremendous city called the "New Jerusalem") and the new earth will replace the old heaven (paradise) and the old earth. They are described in some detail in Chapters 21 and 22. Descriptions of life on the new earth are also provided in Isaiah 65:17-25 and in Ezek. 40-48. The time period covered by this Isaiah passage is established in the starting verse, Isaiah 65:17, which sets the time at the time of the creation of the new heavens and a new earth, according to Rev. 21:1.

In reading this passage from Isaiah 65, it is interesting to note that the citizens of the new earth will live much longer than do the citizens of our earth at the present time. Their lifetimes will be equivalent to the lifetimes of the old Patriarchs – Adam, Seth, Enosh, Cainan, etc., at the time of the first creation. Verse 22 states that they will live to be as old as trees; however, the passage also indicates that they are destined to experience physical death after their long lives on the new earth have been fulfilled. They will not receive the eternal life that will be given only to Christians.

In Rev. 21:24 we read: *"And the nations of those who are saved shall walk in its light* [i.e., in the light of the Holy City], *and the kings of the earth bring their glory and honor into it."* This illustrates the relationship that will exist at that time between the occupants of the new heaven and the new earth – the kings of earth will be allowed to visit the Holy City in the new heaven, but will not reside there permanently. It is interesting to note that the twelve gates to the New Jerusalem will be named for the twelve tribes of Israel, for it is through these gates that the Israelites will pass when they visit the Holy City (see Rev. 21:12-13).

With regard to the Christian residents of the New Jerusalem, Jesus said: *"...I will come again, and receive you to Myself; that where I am, there you may be also."* (John 14:3). Therefore, it seems obvious that all spiritually regenerate Christians will eventually become residents of the New Jerusalem with Christ.

Similarly, any non-Christians or Jews judged to be righteous when Christ judges the nations will remain on earth during the Millennium and perhaps occupy the new earth at a later time, depending upon God's evaluation of their righteousness in His "white throne" judgment. It should be remembered that in His covenants with Abraham, Isaac, and Jacob, God promised the land of Canaan as an everlasting possession for their descendants (see Genesis 17:8; 48:3-4). Therefore, the nation of Israel is destined to remain on the earth (old or new) forever in fulfillment of this promise.

Summary and Conclusions

The topics covered in the preceding discussion can be summarized briefly as follows:

- The primary purpose of the book is to disclose God's plan for redeeming the world from Satan and to present the eschatological prophecies of the Bible in their proper chronological order.

- The first seven chapters are introductory chapters, introducing the author (Christ Jesus), the transcriber (St. John the Divine) and the seven recipient churches in Asia Minor. These chapters also describe John's spiritual visit to God's throne room and God's overall plan for redeeming the world from Satan.

- The remaining 15 chapters, starting with Rev. 8:2, disclose the main apocalyptic message of the book in which all events are listed in chronological order. However, this section contains several chapters that must be regarded as "interlude chapters," giving enlarged details pertaining to certain events but without conforming to the chronological order of the message. These interlude chapters are: Chapters 10, 12-13, 15, 17-18.

In considering the terms of God's redemptive plan, we may be amazed at the intensity of tribulation and suffering that is to be imposed on the human race at the close of the church age. However, this intense suffering is God's way of testing the faith of Christians before taking them into heaven via the harvest rapture. Persecution is considered to be the "fertilizer" that makes the faith of Christians grow strong.

As for those Christians who may be alive on earth during the first six years of the tribulation period, their faith will be severely tested (see Heb. 12:26-29; I Peter 1:6-7). However, they will have no reason to fear these tests as long as they continue to trust God and remain under the protection of His Holy Spirit (see Luke 21:36, Rev. 9:3-4).

Having completed this outline of the Revelation to John, the book can be studied in more detail and, with the help of the Holy Spirit, many valuable insights can be obtained concerning future events. My prayer is that we will all be guided into the same truth, and that the widely differing interpretations of this book will eventually be merged into one true picture of God's program for the redemption of the world.

E. "Berk" Hammond

CLOSING EVENTS OF THE CHURCH AGE

(First released in February 2006)

*   *   *   *   *   *   *

Preface

On the morning of December 31, 2005 God awakened me at 5:30 a.m., and I felt His presence intensely. This was unusual for me, for I normally begin to open my eyes at around 7:00 a.m.

After getting my attention, God began to bring to my memory several verses or passages of scripture with which I was familiar, but which I had not fully understood. Then He began to give me His interpretation of these scriptures and to show me the way in which they were related to each other. After He had completed this training session, He instructed me to prepare a new paper to be distributed to those to whom I would be directed, and the title for the paper was to be: "Closing Events of the Church Age."

The entire month of January, 2006, was spent in preparing this paper under God's direction, and I pray that it will be of real benefit to all those who read it. The scenario that is presented for the close of the church age is quite different from anything that has been taught in our churches for many years, and it might be difficult for some Christians to accept. However, the basic ideas and interpretations that are presented herein were given to me by the Holy Spirit – they are not my own.

*   *   *   *   *   *   *

Contents

- Introduction
- Two Alternate Christian Destinies
- The Purpose and Format of the Revelation to John
- God's Pre-Tribulational Visit to Earth
- The Spiritual Significance of the Baptism with Fire
- Jesus' Resurrection – The Partial Rapture of the Christians
- Jesus' Post-Resurrection Blessing – The Baptism with Fire
- The Post-Resurrection Ministries
- Jesus' Ascension – The Harvest Rapture of the Church
- Comments Concerning the Timing of these Events
- Summary and Conclusions

*   *   *   *   *   *   *

Introduction

To date there have been many different interpretations of scriptural passages that relate to events that God has planned for the closing years of the church age. Most of our church leaders today would probably agree that Christ Jesus will return some day and establish His government over all of the nations of the earth. Perhaps they might also believe that He will visit the earth prior to that time and take some or all of the Christian saints up to heaven in what has been called the "rapture" of the church. However, there is much disagreement among those who accept these concepts concerning the timing of these events. The purpose of this paper is to present a Biblical approach to the study of these questions in order to develop an end-time scenario that should be acceptable to most Christians today.

The approach to be taken in making this study will be based on (1) the Revelation to John, and (2) a statement found in Rev. 19:10 to the effect that *"... the testimony of Jesus is the spirit of prophecy."* The words "the spirit of prophecy" in this passage might be interpreted as the life or the essence of prophecy. This text indicates that as the church age comes to its conclusion, the Christian church collectively will have to experience the major events that Jesus encountered during at least the latter part of His previous life on earth. Since only those events in Jesus' life that have not yet been experienced by the church are of any prophetic significance, they will be addressed in this document and used to generate an end-time scenario.

Two Alternate Christian Destinies

Before exploring the events in Jesus' life that foretell coming events in the life of the church, it will be necessary to examine what the Revelation to John has to say about the final destinies of Christians after they are taken to heaven. The Revelation describes two distinct groups into which Christians will be divided before they enter into heaven (or Paradise). The first tremendously large group is described in Rev. 7:9-17 as Christians who have been taken out of the "great tribulation." Their duties are outlined in Verse 15, which reads as follows: *"Therefore they are before the throne of God, and serve Him day and night in His temple. And He who sits on the throne will dwell among them."* This group can be called God's **"serving"** Christians.

The second group is described in Rev. 20:4, which reads: *"And I saw thrones, and they sat on them, and judgment was committed to them. Then I saw the souls of those who had been beheaded for their witness to Jesus and for the word of God, who had not worshipped the beast or his image, and had not received his mark on their foreheads or on their hands. And they lived and reigned with Christ for a thousand years."* This group can be called Christ's **"ruling"** Christians. These passages of scripture make it quite apparent that the two groups of Christians are mutually exclusive, for there is no way in which a Christian could serve God in His heavenly temple and rule with Christ on earth at the same time.

There is another verse of scripture that indicates the relative size of these two groups. This text is found in Matt. 22:14, which reads as follows: *"For many are called, but few are chosen."* Since this statement is given as an addendum to a parable that describes the selection of individuals for participation in the divine wedding feast in heaven, it seems to refer to the two groups of Christians that have just been identified. This verse could probably be amplified to read: *"For many are called to be serving Christians, but few are chosen to be ruling Christians in Christ's millennial government on earth."* The fact that many are called is supported by Rev. 7:9, which states that the group of serving Christians will be so large that no one can count the number of them. No such statement is made with regard to the ruling Christians.

It is also interesting to note that reference is made to these two groups of Christians in Rev. 17:14, which reads: *"These [the armies of the Antichrist] will make war with the Lamb, and the Lamb will overcome them, for He is Lord of lords and King of kings, and those who are with Him are called, chosen, and faithful."* This passage refers to the battle of Armageddon, which will take place after the final rapture of the church, and it shows that both the called and the chosen groups of Christians will be with Christ at that time. The word "faithful" was apparently added to emphasize the need for Christians to be faithful and to "endure to the end." (see Matt. 24:13)

This division of responsibilities of the saints in heaven may come as quite a surprise to many Christians who have been taught that after Christians are removed from the earth they will constitute one unified group. However, the texts quoted above from the Revelation do not support this idea. Just as the Holy Spirit decides which of the various spiritual gifts to give to each Christian, God also decides which Christians are needed to be servants to Him in His temple in heaven, and which ones are needed to assist Christ Jesus in governing the people of the earth during the Millennium. Remember that God is a sovereign God, and that He said: *"... My ways are higher than your ways, and My thoughts than your thoughts."* (Isaiah 55:9)

It will be well to keep these two groups of Christians in mind, for the events to which they will be exposed at the close of the church age will be quite different. Both groups will eventually arrive at the same place – the New Jerusalem – but the paths that they will travel to get there will be quite different.

The Purpose and Format of the Revelation to John

Since the Revelation to John describes most of the events that will take place at and following the close of the church age, it is advisable to consider the purpose for which it was written, and also its format. A discussion of these topics is presented in another of my articles entitled "An Introduction to the Revelation to John," and for the sake of brevity it will not be repeated here. However, a brief summary of the conclusions that were reached is as follows.

The purpose of the Book of Revelation is given in Rev. 1:1 as follows: "*The Revelation of Jesus Christ, which God gave Him to show His servants — things which must shortly take place. And He sent and signified it by His angel to His servant John.*" Thus the purpose is: (1) to present and disclose to God's servants His plan for redeeming the world from Satan, and (2) to present a scenario of future eschatological events in their proper chronological order (1-7 seals, 1-7 trumpets, 1-7 bowls of God's wrath, etc.). Furthermore, in Rev. 22:18-19 severe punishment is promised for anyone who changes any of the words of this book.

As for the format of the book, it is divided into two primary sections, each having several sub-sections as follows:

Section I – The Introduction

1. Chapter 1 – God is proclaimed as the true author of the book and Jesus as the One to pass His messages on to John, the writer.

2. Chapters 2-3 – These chapters introduce the seven churches to whom the book is to be sent.

3. Chapters 4-5 – John's visit to God's throne room in heaven is described here.

4. Chapter 6 – This chapter introduces (1) the four demonic spirits that will be released to torment the citizens of earth during the entire life of the church, (2) the Christian martyrs, and (3) the severe cataclysmic events that will be encountered during the tribulation period.

5. Chapter 7 – Two major events that will occur during the tribulation period are described in this chapter. They are: (1) the selection of the special 144,000 Jewish bond-servants to be transported into heaven, and (2) the final harvest rapture of the Christian saints.

Section 2 – The Apocalyptic Message

1. Chapters 8-18 describe in detail events that will take place on earth during the tribulation period. These events are listed in chronological order.

2. Chapter 19 lists the events that will take place in heaven following the final harvest rapture of the church.

3. Chapter 20 outlines briefly the series of post-tribulational events that are destined to occur during the time of Christ's millennial reign on earth.

4. Chapters 21 and 22 describe the wonders of the new heaven and the new earth, which will replace the old heaven and the old earth after they are destroyed.

From this outline, it is apparent that in order to explore the timing of any events of the tribulation period, their descriptions must first be found in Chapters 8-18.

God's Pre-Tribulational Visit to Earth

The sounding of the first tribulational trumpet in Rev. 8:7 marks the beginning of the final seven-year period of tribulation, but from Rev. 8:3-5 it is apparent that there is a series of very special supernatural events that will precede the start of the tribulation. These verses read as follows:

> *(3) Then another angel, having a golden censer, came and stood at the altar. He was given much incense, that he should offer it with the prayers of all the saints upon the golden altar which was before the throne.*
> *(4) And the smoke of the incense, with the prayers of the saints, ascended before God from the angel's hand.*

(5) Then the angel took the censer, filled it with fire from the altar, and threw it to the earth. And there were noises, thunderings, lightnings, and an earthquake.

This is not an easy passage to interpret, but whatever the events described in this passage may be, it is obvious that they will happen just before the tribulation period begins.

The action part of this passage is contained in Verse 5. The event described therein will be initiated when an angel throws fire from the altar in heaven down to the earth, and this would seem to be a "baptism with fire" for the citizens of earth who receive it. Remember also that John the Baptist predicted a "baptism with fire" to follow the baptism with the Holy Spirit in Matt. 3:11 and in Luke 3:16.

The Spiritual Significance of the Baptism with Fire

It seems that the baptism with fire may be similar to Holy Spirit baptism as it was experienced by the first disciples at Pentecost, in that tongues of fire may fall on those who have been chosen to receive this baptism. But what will be the differences between these two baptisms?

At the time of creation, the Holy Trinity consisted of three divine Beings – God the Father, the "Word," and the Holy Spirit – and each of these was a spiritual Being. It is difficult to differentiate between these three spiritual Beings except on the basis of their functions. God the Father was the architect for the universe, the "Word" (the Spirit of Christ Jesus – John 1:1,14) was the builder (see John 1:3; Col. 1:15-16), and the Holy Spirit provided the spiritual power needed to support the building process.

John the Baptist said that Christ Jesus would give us two baptisms – a baptism with the Holy Spirit and a baptism with fire. As of today many Christians have received the baptism with the Holy Spirit, giving them the necessary spiritual power to combat the evils of this world and to live a victorious life here on earth. However, the baptism with fire is yet to come.

Some believe that the baptism with fire simply refers to the suffering and persecution (demonic or otherwise) that Christians can expect to encounter after receiving the baptism with the Holy Spirit. However, it is not likely that anyone has received the baptism with fire as of this time. Since the baptism with the Holy Spirit occurred initially as a single supernatural event, then it seems likely that the baptism with fire will occur in a similar fashion, in just the way that it is described in Rev. 8:5.

According to Hebrews 12:29, *"... our God is a consuming fire."* Also, in Deut. 4:24 we are told: *"For the Lord your God is a consuming fire, a jealous God."* It seems clear that the name "God" in these verses refers to God the Father, the God of Israel and the spiritual Father of all born-again Christians. Therefore, being baptized with fire from the altar in heaven (as in Rev. 8:5) must mean being baptized with the Spirit of God the Father. The ruling Christians who are chosen to receive this baptism will receive the love, wisdom and other major characteristics of God the Father, thus qualifying them to become rulers under Christ Jesus during the Millennium.

According to Rev. 8:5, the baptism with fire will be accompanied by *"noises, thunderings, lightnings, and an earthquake."* It should be noted that except for the earthquake, these audible and visual signs are identical to those that St. John the Divine experienced when he was allowed to visit God's throne room in heaven (see Rev. 4:5). Exod. 20:18 discloses that these events were also experienced when God visited Moses and the children of Israel on Mount Sinai. Therefore it is apparent that *"noises, thunderings, and lightnings"* are true signs of the presence of God the Father at the place they are experienced. The earthquake mentioned in Rev. 8:5 apparently indicates how the earth will tremble at the presence of Almighty God.

Now that the supernatural event preceding the final seven-year tribulation period has been identified, the scriptures that show how this experience relates to Jesus' testimony can be explored.

The first event in Jesus' life that has not yet been experienced by the church is His death on the cross. Although it may not be pleasant to consider, all Christians will have to die physically before they can be taken into Paradise, via either a rapture event or a natural death. However, Jesus' tragic death on the cross was an event that only He will ever have to endure. It was an event that brought salvation and eternal life to those who would subsequently yield their lives to Him and believe in Him.

Jesus is the only One qualified to sacrifice His life to remove the sins of future believers. Therefore, members of the Christian church will not be required to experience a tragic event of this magnitude in the future, and for this all Christians may be thankful!

Subsequent to His crucifixion, Jesus spent three days in Hades and, according to 1 Peter 3:18-20, He preached to the souls of some of the residents of Hades during that time. His visit to Hades was apparently necessary to liberate Him from the sins of the world that He had taken upon Himself, so that He could return to earth via His resurrection. However, Christians do not have such a sin burden to be removed; their sins have been forgiven as a result of their belief in their Savior, Christ Jesus. Therefore, Christians should not have to experience a trip to Hades, as Jesus did.

The remaining events in Christ Jesus' life on earth that the Christians who have been chosen to be rulers will have to experience are:

- His resurrection
- His receipt of God's post-resurrection blessing
- His 40-day post-resurrection ministry to His disciples
- His ascension into heaven

Jesus' Resurrection – The Partial Rapture of the Christians

The first supernatural event that Jesus experienced following His death on the cross was His resurrection from the dead. For Christians, the event that seems to duplicate this experience best is the rapture of the church, described by Paul in 1 Thess. 4:13-17 and in 1 Cor. 15:51-52. However, in another of my recent studies, I noted that there will be two different future rapture events – (1) a partial rapture, and (2) a final harvest rapture. Jesus predicted the partial rapture in Matt. 24:40-43 and in Luke 17:34-37, and the harvest rapture is described in 1 Thess. 4:13-17, John 6:39-40 and Rev. 14:14-16.

In case there is any concern about the fact that the word "rapture" does not occur in the Bible, I offer a brief description of the origin of this word. The Biblical passage that is quoted most often in connection with the rapture is 1 Thess. 4:13-17, which tells how Christians will eventually be "caught up" to meet Christ Jesus in the air supernaturally. The Greek word *"harpazo,"* used in the original text, was translated as the English verb "caught up." However, in the Latin Vulgate Version of the Bible, the Latin word *"raptos"* replaced the Greek word *"harpazo,"* and it is from this Latin word that the English word "rapture" is derived.

In the partial rapture, only the Christians chosen to be ruling Christians will be taken, and all other Christians will be left on earth to be taken in the final harvest rapture, about six years later. However, in either of these two events, the Christians who are taken will die physically, just as Jesus did, and they will be given spiritual bodies similar to Jesus' post-resurrection body. In 1 John 3:2, John is quoted as saying: *"Beloved, now we are children of God; and it has not yet been revealed what we shall be, but we know that when He is revealed, we shall be like Him, for we shall see Him as He is."*

Since there will be no further use for the physical bodies of the raptured Christians, they will be left on earth as food for the eagles (see Matt. 24:27-28 and Luke 17:37). However, please note that this will be one event that is not in accordance with the testimony of Jesus. Presumably, Jesus' physical body was actually changed into a spiritual body, since His body did not remain in His grave. This was apparently necessary in order to prove to those who saw His wounds that He was really the risen Christ Jesus. Furthermore, He had committed no sins while living in His physical body, so there was no reason for it to be discarded.

Jesus' Post-Resurrection Blessing – The Baptism with Fire

Immediately following His resurrection, Jesus had a conversation with Mary Magdalene that is recorded in John 20:14-17. In Verse 17, Jesus told Mary: *"… Do not cling to Me, for I have not yet ascended to My Father; but go to My brethren and say to them, 'I am ascending to My Father and your Father, and to My God and your God.'"* He did not give a reason for having to ascend to heaven and meet with His Father, but He probably needed to receive a blessing from Him prior to continuing His ministry on earth and thereafter.

In this verse Mary was told not to cling to Jesus, but from John 20:26-27 it is apparent that when Jesus met with His disciples in the upper room at a later time Thomas was invited to touch His wounds. Therefore we may conclude that at some time between His conversation with Mary and His visit to the upper room He did ascend to heaven to meet with His Father and receive a special blessing from Him.

When the ruling Christians are taken in the partial rapture and given the baptism with fire, the blessing that they will receive will no doubt be similar to the blessing that Jesus must have received when He first ascended to God the Father after His resurrection. The "chosen" Christians will receive a special blessing from God, enabling them to serve as rulers under Christ Jesus during the Millennium. This blessing is expected to be the result of their "baptism with fire," and they will be made into powerful "sons of God" at that time (see Rom. 8:19).

The Post-Resurrection Ministries

After spending three days in Hades, Jesus was resurrected and brought back to live on earth for forty days. During that time, He met with His disciples on several occasions, encouraging them, exhorting them, and teaching them things that they needed to know. There seems to be no record of His talking with anyone other than His disciples during this period of time.

In a similar fashion the ruling Christian candidates are likely to be left on earth as spiritual ministers after being baptized with fire, having the same kind of bodies that Jesus had following His resurrection. It is likely that they will be expected to advise, assist, encourage, exhort and teach the serving Christians that were left on earth at the time of the partial rapture. Considering the fact that these serving Christians will be living under the rule of the Antichrist, they should welcome any help that can be provided by their spiritual brothers and sisters.

Although Jesus remained on earth for only forty days before His ascension into heaven, it is likely that the ruling Christian candidates will continue their ministry for approximately six years, until the entire Christian church is removed from the earth via the final harvest rapture.

Jesus' Ascension –
The Harvest Rapture of the Church

After spending forty days on earth ministering to His disciples, Jesus ascended into heaven and disappeared into a cloud (see Acts 1:4-9). The description of His ascension is similar in many ways to Paul's description of the rapture (the catching up) of the Christian saints given in 1 Thess. 4:13-18. Therefore, it seems reasonable to conclude that the final rapture of the church corresponds to Jesus' ascension to heaven.

This final rapture event is pictured quite clearly in Rev. 14:14-16 and, since it describes the harvesting of wheat (representing Christians), it has been called the "harvest" rapture. It will occur after the last (the seventh) tribulational trumpet has been sounded (in Rev. 11:15), but before the outpouring of the seven bowls of God's wrath, described in Chapter 16.

The description of this rapture event in Rev. 14 contains no hint of a judgment or a selection process. Therefore we may conclude that this rapture represents the fulfillment of Jesus' statement given in John 6:39: *"This is the will of the Father who sent Me, that of all He has given Me I should lose nothing, but should raise it up at the last day."* When this harvest rapture occurs, all ruling and serving Christians will be taken to heaven, and no true Christians will be left behind. Immediately following this rapture, the previous works of the raptured Christians will be judged at the judgment seat of Christ (see 2 Cor. 5:10).

Comments Concerning the Timing of these Events

With regard to the timing of the final events that have been predicted for the church, only our sovereign God in heaven knows just when they will occur. That being the case, why would it be necessary to estimate or even consider the schedule which God has set for these events?

It seems that some consideration should be given to the probable timing of these events in order to evaluate the importance of the teachings that have been given. If the occurrence of these events could be shown to be imminent, then the teachings would be of much more concern to the readers than if their occurrences were thought to be remote. For this reason, some consideration should be given to any scriptures that relate to the approximate timing of this series of events.

The timing of these events was explored in some detail in another of my articles titled "God's Three Special Levitical Feasts," and for the sake of brevity only the conclusions presented in that document will be given here. It was shown that the harvest rapture and the Second Coming of Christ Jesus are each likely to occur during a Jewish Feast of Tabernacles celebration, but in different years.

As for the partial rapture, it will probably occur around the time of a Pentecost celebration because the subsequent baptism with fire will be similar in many respects to the baptism with the Holy Spirit received at Pentecost around 2,000 years ago. As for the year in which the partial rapture will take place, only God knows the year in which it is destined to occur.

Please do not let this discussion of the timing of these events detract in any way from the basic message of the article concerning the sequence of the end-time events. Regardless of when they begin, I believe that they will definitely occur quite soon and in accordance with the scenario that has been presented.

Summary and Conclusions

Before investigating prophecies that relate to the future of the Christian church it was necessary to recognize that the church is composed of two separate and distinct groups – the ruling Christians and the serving Christians. The ruling Christians are those who have been chosen to reign with Christ on the earth during the Millennium (see Rev. 20:4), and the serving Christians are those who have been called to serve God in His temple in heaven (see Rev. 7:9-17). Both groups will eventually arrive at the same destination following Christ's millennial rule on earth, at the tremendous city called the "New Jerusalem," described in Rev. 21:9-27. However, the routes that they will take to reach this destination will be quite different.

The angel's declaration, contained in Rev. 19:10, to the effect that *"the testimony of Jesus is the spirit of prophecy,"* leads to the conclusion that the major prophetic events to be experienced by the church at the close of the church age will be similar to those experienced by Jesus, beginning in the week of His crucifixion. On this basis, a scenario for the close of the church age was developed.

Some of the predicted events will be experienced only by those persons chosen to be ruling Christians, and other events relate to the called Christians. However, the prophecies concerning the final harvest rapture of the Christian saints apply to both ruling and serving Christians alike. It appears that before any Christian who has been chosen to be a ruling Christian can take his or her position as a member of Christ's government during the Millennium, the person must first experience the major events that Jesus faced during the latter part of His first visit to earth.

The primary events predicted for ruling Christians in the future are:

1. The Partial Rapture

Corresponding to Jesus' death and resurrection the ruling Christians are expected to experience the partial rapture, in which their physical bodies will be translated to a remote location on earth and replaced by spiritual bodies, similar to the body that Jesus had following His resurrection. Their dead physical bodies will be left on the earth as food for the eagles or vultures. At this time other ruling Christian candidates who died prior to this time will join them.

Since these chosen Christians are destined to rule over certain assigned areas of the earth during the Millennium, it is quite possible that they may be sent to their assigned areas of jurisdiction. In that way they would be able to become familiar with the life and customs of those living in their assigned areas before being told to rule over them.

2. The Baptism with Fire

The baptism with fire – prophesied by John the Baptist in Matt. 3:11 and Luke 3:16 and described in Rev. 8:5 – will give those persons chosen to be ruling Christians the love, wisdom and other characteristics of God the Father (the "consuming fire"). This will enable them to adequately perform their duties as ruling Christians under Christ during the Millennium.

3. The Final Exit via the Harvest Rapture

After the seventh tribulational trumpet has been sounded about six years after the start of the tribulation, both the ruling and serving Christians will be taken to heaven via the harvest rapture (described in Rev. 14:14-16), just as Jesus was taken up on the day of His ascension. Therefore, no true Christians will be left alive on earth when the seven bowls of God's wrath are poured out on the inhabitants of earth during the final year of the tribulation period.

It may seem unfair to make the serving Christians suffer through the events of six years of the tribulation while the ruling Christians are allowed to move into the spiritual world before the tribulation begins.

However, many Christians seem to be going through intense periods of suffering at the present time, and some pastors have observed that this suffering seems to be heaviest for the most devout Christians. Could it be that those who are suffering the most now are the ruling Christian candidates who will escape the tribulation, and that those who are suffering the least now are the serving Christians who will suffer the events of the tribulation at a later time? Only God knows the answer to this question.

Since the events listed above have been derived on the basis of Jesus' testimony while He was alive on earth and immediately thereafter, it must end with His ascension, corresponding to the final harvest rapture of the entire Christian church. As for the timing of this rapture event, only our sovereign God in heaven knows the exact day on which it will occur.

The events that Christians will experience following the harvest rapture are covered in Revelation, Chapters 19-20. These chapters reveal that immediately following this rapture the ruling Christians will be bonded to Jesus in a divine wedding ceremony.

Since the Christian martyrs are shown in Rev. 6:9 to be residing under the altar in heaven, they most likely constitute the true bride of Christ. They are uniquely qualified for this position because they have given their lives for Christ Jesus, just as He gave His life for them and for us at Calvary. The other ruling Christians, excluding the martyrs, must then constitute the body of Christ.

It is interesting to note that, except in the book of Revelation, the church is never referred to as the bride of Christ; instead, it is called the body of Christ (see Rom. 12:4-5). Apparently this is because prior to a Christian's death, there is no way to know whether or not he or she will be qualified to be a part of Christ's bride through martyrdom.

This distinction between the bride and the body of Christ can only be made prior to the time of the divine marriage ceremony, for at that time the body and the bride will "become one flesh," and will no longer be distinguishable one from the other. As for the serving Christians, they are likely to be invited to the marriage supper as guests of the Bridegroom (see Rev. 19:9). After the wedding ceremony has ended, the ruling Christians will return to earth with Jesus to assist in establishing His millennial kingdom, and the serving Christians will begin to serve God in His heavenly temple.

Christ Jesus' kingdom on earth will exist for 1,000 years, after which a new heaven and a new earth will replace the old heaven and the old earth. The new heaven will contain an enormous city called the "New Jerusalem," which will be the final home for both the ruling and the serving Christians.

The scenario presented herein is believed to be quite different from any being taught today in our churches. However, it has been presented in just the way that it was received, and it is my prayer that the Holy Spirit will reveal the truth about the final events of the church age to all those who read this document. Its purpose is to prepare all Christians for the supernatural events to come, so that they will understand their significance when they occur.

May God bless all those who read this document, and may He make it a means for bringing more unity into His church.

E. "Berk" Hammond

GOD'S THREE SPECIAL LEVITICAL FEASTS
(First released in August 2010)

*   *   *   *   *   *   *

The Bible Book of Leviticus describes seven special times of celebration or feasting that the Jews are required to observe each year. Since they are described in Leviticus, they have been called the Levitical feasts, or celebrations. They are as follows:

1.   The Passover Supper

2.   The Feast of Unleavened Bread

3.   The Feast of First Fruits

4.   The Feast of Pentecost (or Weeks)

5.   The Feast of Trumpets

6.   The Day of Atonement

7.   The Feast of Tabernacles (or Booths)

With the exception of the Day of Atonement, all of these celebrations involve feasting to some degree.

Although God has stated that all seven of these celebrations are important and have a role to play in the Jewish faith, He has identified three of them as being of special significance. These are identified in Deut. 16:16 as follows: *"Three times a year all your males shall appear before the* LORD *your God in the place which He chooses: at the Feast of Unleavened Bread, at the Feast of Weeks, and at the Feast of Tabernacles; and they shall not appear before the* LORD *empty-handed."* Thus it is apparent that the feasts of Unleavened Bread, Weeks, and Tabernacles are especially important to God. His selection of these three feasts is also confirmed in 2 Chron. 8:13. Of course, God always has good reasons for all of His actions, and His reason for emphasizing the importance of these three Levitical feasts will now be investigated.

It has always been God's plan to create a Christian church as a bride for His Son Jesus, and it will be shown that these three special Levitical feasts relate in some way to the formation and the destiny of this Christian church. Before this church could be formed, it was necessary for Jesus to be put to death to atone for the sins of those who choose to follow Him and become members of His church. Then, three days after His death, He was resurrected to become the leader of His new church. It is significant to note that Jesus' resurrection occurred during a Feast of Unleavened Bread, thus providing Christian fulfillment for the first of the three special Levitical feasts.

The second step in the formation of the Christian church was to give its members spiritual power and gifts as needed to carry out their assignments on earth and to function in accordance with God's plans. It is also significant to note that this action was taken during a Feast of Weeks (Pentecost), the second of the three special Levitical feasts. At that time the Holy Spirit came and filled each church member with His spiritual power, and this is considered to be the birthday of the Christian church. This can also be considered to be a Christian fulfillment for the Feast of Weeks.

It is apparent that the first two of the three Levitical feasts have already been given at least partial Christian fulfillment, but the third feast – the Feast of Tabernacles – remains to be fulfilled. There are only two future church-related events that can be considered as candidates for the Christian fulfillment of the Feast of Tabernacles celebration – (1) the partial rapture of the ruling Christians and (2) the harvest rapture, in which Christ Jesus will take **all** Christians into heaven to attend His divine marriage ceremony, leaving the earth completely devoid of any true Christians (see 1 Cor. 15:51-52; 1 Thess. 4:13-18; Rev. 14:14-16). It is now necessary to determine whether these two rapture events qualify for the Christian fulfillment of the Feast of Tabernacles.

The first step in this process will be to determine the real meaning and significance of the Feast of Tabernacles. This is explained in Lev. 23:42-43, which reads as follows: *"You shall dwell in booths for seven days. All who are native Israelites shall dwell in booths, that your generations may know that I made the children of Israel dwell in booths when I brought them out of the land of Egypt: I am the LORD your God."* Therefore, the purpose of this feast is to remind the Jews of the time at which God used His supernatural power to bring them out of their bondage in the land of Egypt.

It seems that any event that is to be considered as a Christian fulfillment for the Feast of Tabernacles should bear some resemblance to the event that the feast represents – God's supernatural deliverance of the Jews from Egyptian bondage. Considering the harvest rapture mentioned above, it seems that it has a purpose similar to that of the exodus from Egypt – i.e., to deliver all true Christians from the tyranny of the Antichrist, just as the Jews were delivered from the tyranny of the Egyptian Pharaoh. Therefore, it seems safe to assume that the harvest rapture is destined to occur during a future Feast of Tabernacles.

As for the partial rapture, its purpose will be to collect the "chosen" Christians and prepare them for their future work as rulers under Christ Jesus. The subsequent baptism with fire will qualify these ruling Christians for their future roles as rulers under Christ, and the partial rapture will also serve to protect them from persecution by the Antichrist. Therefore, because this protection is similar to that provided to the Jews in their exodus from Egypt, it seems reasonable to conclude that the partial rapture will also occur during the time of a future Feast of Tabernacles.

The two raptures are church-related events, whereas Jesus' Second Coming has no relationship to the Christian church, which will have been moved into heaven previously via the harvest rapture. However, the prophet Zechariah addressed this problem with his prophecy given in Zech. 14:16, which reads as follows: *"And it shall come to pass that everyone who is left of all the nations which came against Jerusalem shall go up from year to year to worship the King, the LORD of hosts, and to keep the Feast of Tabernacles."*

Zechariah's message is directed to those living on the earth subsequent to the battle of Armageddon (i.e., to non-Christian Gentiles and Jews). The most likely reason that non-Christian Gentiles would have for celebrating the Feast of Tabernacles would be to commemorate the time at which Christ Jesus had arrived on earth as their King. Therefore it seems safe to conclude that the partial rapture, the harvest rapture, and the Second Coming of Christ will each occur during a future Feast of Tabernacles, but in different years.

The Bible does not indicate the specific year in which the partial rapture will occur, but there are many reasons to believe that its occurrence is imminent. Let us all be ready!

E. "Berk" Hammond

TARES IN THE WHEAT FIELD
(First released in August 1990)

*   *   *   *   *   *   *

Contents

- The Basic Parable of the Tares in the Wheat Field
- Jesus' Interpretation of the Parable
- Parables and Allegories
- The Significance of God's Book of Life
- Analyzing the Parable
- Biblical Examples of Tares
- Summary and Conclusions

*   *   *   *   *   *   *

The Basic Parable of the Tares in the Wheat Field

Jesus' parable of the tares (or weeds) in the wheat field is perhaps the most controversial of all His parables. Even though Jesus Himself explains it fully, His explanation is quite difficult for some people to accept. However, we must remember that God is sovereign, which means that He can do anything He wishes to do, at any time He desires, in any way that He wants, and without asking our permission.

After reading this paper, many will say to themselves, "Surely there must be another more palatable interpretation that can be found for this parable other than the one given in this paper!" This thought crossed my mind also when God first gave me this interpretation, but when I asked Him for confirmation He assured me that the explanation that I had received was correct in every detail, and that I should not change it in any way. Therefore, I am being obedient to His instructions, and I am presenting the interpretation just as it was given to me.

This parable, found in Matthew 13:24-30, reads as follows:

> *(24) Another parable He put forth to them, saying: "The kingdom of heaven is like a man who sowed good seed in his field;*
> *(25) but while men slept, his enemy came and sowed tares among the wheat and went his way.*
> *(26) But when the grain had sprouted and produced a crop, then the tares also appeared.*
> *(27) So the servants of the owner came and said to him, 'Sir, did you not sow good seed in your field? How then does it have tares?'*
> *(28) He said to them, 'An enemy has done this.' The servants said to him, 'Do you want us then to go and gather them up?'*
> *(29) But he said, 'No, lest while you gather up the tares you also uproot the wheat with them.'"*

Jesus' Interpretation of the Parable

The above verses present the parable in its original form, but since His disciples apparently could not understand its meaning, Jesus interpreted it for them. His interpretation, given in Verses 37-43, reads as follows:

> *(37) He answered and said to them: "He who sows the good seed is the Son of Man.*
> *(38) The field is the world, the good seeds are the sons of the kingdom, but the tares are the sons of the wicked one.*
> *(39) The enemy who sowed them is the devil, the harvest is the end of the age, and the reapers are the angels.*
> *(40) Therefore as the tares are gathered and burned in the fire, so it will be at the end of this age.*
> *(41) The Son of Man will send out His angels, and they will gather out of His kingdom all things that offend, and those who practice lawlessness,*
> *(42) and will cast them into the furnace of fire. There will be wailing and gnashing of teeth.*
> *(43) Then the righteous will shine forth as the sun in the kingdom of their Father. He who has ears to hear, let him hear!"*

In these explanatory verses Jesus clearly states that not everyone who is born on this earth is a potential child of God's kingdom. Some persons are children of the evil one and, for reasons that will be discussed later, they can never become children of God or citizens of His kingdom. This fact is difficult for many to accept, but we should remember that God's ways are not our ways (see Isaiah 55:8-9).

Remember also that Verses 37-43 from Matthew 13 given above do not present a second parable; they simply provide Jesus' own interpretation of His parable of the tares. Therefore, we have no right or reason to reinterpret His interpretation of this parable. However, before analyzing this parable further, let us consider the definition and the purpose of any parable.

Parables and Allegories

Harper's Bible Dictionary contains a brief article on parables in which a parable is defined as "a short fictitious narrative based on a familiar experience and having an application to the spiritual life." In this same article, an allegory is defined as "a symbolic narrative in which every detail has a figurative meaning." There are some who believe that Jesus' parables are not to be considered as allegories. However, in the case of the parable of the tares in the wheat field, I cannot accept this belief as being true, for Jesus certainly did interpret this parable as an allegory.

In explaining the message of this parable, Jesus gave a figurative meaning to every detail of the parable, thus classifying it as an allegorical parable (see Verses 37-39). The same is true for His parable of the sower (see Matthew 13:3-9, 18-23). From Jesus' explanation of these two parables, it seems obvious that He intended that at least these two parables, and perhaps all of His parables, should be interpreted as allegories.

Before the meaning of any allegorical parable can be fully understood, a code must be established which shows the relationship between the objects and activities in the story and those in the heavenly kingdom. The allegorical code given by Jesus for His parable of the tares in the wheat field is as follows:

Item in the Parable	Corresponding Spiritual Item
The sower of good seed	The Son of Man (Jesus)
The field	The world
The good seed	The sons of the kingdom
The tares (or weeds)	The sons of the evil one (Satan)
The sower of bad seed	The devil (Satan)
The time of harvest	The end of the church age
The reapers	The Angels

Jesus' disciples once asked Him why He spoke to the people in parables, and He said that although His disciples had been granted the ability to understand at least some of the mysteries of the kingdom of heaven, ordinary people do not have this ability (see Matthew 13:10-17). Therefore, Jesus used stories involving familiar items, in which the relationship between the items and activities portrayed in the story are similar to the relationship existing between the corresponding items and activities in the kingdom of heaven. These stories, or parables, could therefore be used to explain the details of the heavenly kingdom to those who would otherwise be unable to understand them.

The Significance of God's Book of Life

In His explanation of this parable, Jesus showed that the citizens of earth can be divided into two separate groups: (1) the sons of the kingdom of heaven, and (2) the sons of the evil one (sons of Satan). The first group, consisting primarily of potentially righteous Jews and Gentiles, some of whom are also potential Christians, is often referred to in the Bible as God's "elect"; and the second group can be classified as God's "non-elect," or the human "tares." In order to provide a record of the names of the persons in His elect group, God has written their names in a book, which He called His "Book of Life."

The Bible contains seven references to God's Book of Life, and from Revelation 20:15 and 21:27 it is evident that a person's name must be recorded in this book if he or she is to be saved from destruction in the lake of fire. Rev. 13:8 also reads as follows: *"All who dwell on the earth will worship him, whose names have not been written in the Book of Life of the Lamb slain from the foundation of the world."* It can be seen by inference that: (a) there must be some persons on earth whose names have not been entered into the Book of Life, and (b) those names that are contained in it were entered there at the time of the creation of the world.

Many today believe that a Christian's name is entered in the Book of Life at his or her time of conversion, but according to these latter two verses, no one's name can be entered in this book during or subsequent to his life on earth. Conversely, the statements contained in Revelation 3:5 and in Exodus 32:33 lead to the conclusion that a person could have his or her name erased from the book under certain conditions that might justify such action by God. Then in Luke 10:20, Jesus is recorded as saying to His disciples that those who have experienced salvation and the power of the Holy Spirit should rejoice that their names have been recorded in this book in heaven.

Thus we see that at the time of creation, God made a complete list of all of the persons who would constitute His elect group, and He entered their names in His Book of Life as a record of their election. This makes them eligible for His salvation, provided that they choose to respond to His invitation when it is given. God's pre-selection of the persons destined to be members of His elect group in no way contradicts the fact that He allows everyone to have free choice, for He wants His children to enter the kingdom of heaven by their own free will, and not as robots.

With regard to Christian salvation, Jesus advised His disciples, saying, *"No one can come to Me, unless the Father who sent Me draws him; ..." (John 6:44).* From this it is obvious that God the Father must make the first move by drawing, or inviting, those in His Christian elect group to accept Jesus as their Savior and be "born again" (spiritually regenerated). After the invitation is given, it is the responsibility of the person to accept it and yield to the leadership of Christ.

This sequence of events is clearly illustrated in Jesus' parable of the large dinner (see Luke 14:15-24). This dinner probably symbolizes the future "marriage supper of the Lamb," described in Revelation 19:1-9, which only the Christian elect will be allowed to attend. According to this parable the host, representing God the Father, extended invitations to those that He expected to be present, but His invitation was rejected by many of them because they found it inconvenient to attend. Then in the concluding Verse 24 the host declared: *"For I tell you, none of those men who were invited shall taste of my dinner."*

In studying this latter parable in its spiritual dimension, it seems logical to assume that because of their rejection of God's invitation to attend His banquet, their names may have been removed from His Book of Life, but in any case they will be forbidden to attend the marriage supper of the Lamb. We may also conclude that the final list of names in God's Book of Life will be somewhat shorter than it was at the time of creation, due to the many deletions.

The fact that God wrote the names of all of His elect in His Book of Life at the time of creation leads to some interesting conclusions. Before one of His elect can be born, the parents must be brought together in marriage, which means that each marriage that leads to the birth of an elect son or daughter must also have been preordained at the time of creation. If, in the exercise of their free choice, either of the two chosen parents decides to marry the wrong person, then the elect son or daughter will not be born as planned and his or her name might have to be erased from the Book of Life. Therefore, it is extremely important for Christians to seek God's will before choosing a partner in marriage.

Considering the fact that marriages and conceptions must all have been planned by God as a prerequisite to the birth one of His elect, and also considering the large number of the marriages and conceptions today that were not planned by God, then the number of human "tares" in the world should be large in comparison to the number of God's elect. It was the same in Noah's time, when the world was overrun by the *"Nephilim"* (see Genesis 6). We are reminded of this fact In Luke 17:26-27, which reads: *"And as it was in the days of Noah, so it will be also in the days of the Son of Man: they ate, they drank, they married wives, they were given in marriage, until the day that Noah entered the ark, and the flood came and destroyed them all."*

In addition to the Christian elect, the elect from the nation Israel (and possibly from other nations) are also recorded in the Book of Life (see Exodus 32:31-33; Psalm 69:28; Psalm 139:15-16). Thus we may conclude that the Book of Life contains the names of all those who were ordained to be born on earth as potential citizens of God's kingdom, whether in the new heaven or on the new earth. These elect persons were ordained and named in accordance with His extensive plans for the world and its inhabitants, which He made at the time of creation. Of course, it goes without saying that these elect persons must not give God any reason to erase their names from His book because of any unforgivable deeds (for example, blasphemy against the Holy Spirit – see Matthew 12:32).

The children of Israel were originally and are today a race chosen by God (see Isaiah 44:1-5). When He determined the list of names to be included in His Book of Life, God exercised His sovereign authority. However, from Proverbs 16:4 it is apparent that He makes even the wicked (the non-elect) for the day of evil, thus it is apparent that He gives birth to everyone – to the good and the evil alike.

Analyzing the Parable

In our search for an explanation for this parable, it would seem reasonable to us as human beings that the "sons of the evil one" are often considered to be those persons who have not yet entered the heavenly kingdom by being "born again," but who are eligible to enter the kingdom if and when they accept Jesus as their Savior and Lord. In a certain sense, such persons might possibly be considered to be "sons of the evil one" because Satan probably has been leading them in their dealings with other people. However, this explanation cannot be the correct one, for if it is possible for "sons of the evil one" to later become "sons of the kingdom," then it would have to be possible for the tares (or weeds) of the parable to become wheat plants. We know that in everyday life, tares can never become wheat plants; therefore neither can the sons of the evil one ever become sons of God's kingdom.

As was previously stated, those who are born on this earth as potential children of God's kingdom (His "elect") are therefore eligible to enter His kingdom by accepting His invitation when it is offered. Conversely, any persons who might be children of the devil (the "non-elect" group) would never be eligible for Christian salvation. It might be surprising to some that God would place anyone on this earth who is not eligible for salvation, but Proverbs 16:4 tells us that *"The Lord has made everything for its own purpose, even the wicked for the day of evil."* Therefore, we should not be surprised to find members of the non-elect group in our midst from time to time.

In explaining this parable to His disciples, Jesus stated that the tares symbolize the "sons of the evil one" – not his disciples or followers, but sons of the evil one. However, He did not explain the procedure by which they came to be present on the earth. It is quite likely that God has established an immutable law such that whenever a human sperm cell and an egg cell unite, whether the union was in accordance with His original plan or not, a new person will be born. If this union was in consonance with His will, then the new person will be one of His elect. If it was contrary to His will, the new person will join the non-elect group. This explanation seems to be in agreement with the passage quoted in the previous paragraph.

There are of course some passages of scripture (e.g., 1 Timothy 2:3-6 and Hebrews 2:9) stating that Jesus died for all men and that He wants all men to be saved. This is a true statement in the sense that Jesus' death on the cross for the atonement of the sins of mankind had no limitations. However, according to John 6:44 and 65, there is still another condition that must be met prior to receiving Christian salvation – the person must be drawn to Jesus by God the Father through the gift of faith for salvation (see Ephesians 2:8-9). Obviously, God would not draw a member of the non-elect group to Jesus, since those persons are not eligible for salvation.

Considering the fact that any candidate for salvation must have his or her name recorded in the Book of Life, then there would be absolutely no reason for God to grant faith for salvation to a member of the non-elect group whose name would not be listed in this book, even though Jesus' atonement for the sins of believers was not limited in any way.

The decision as to who is and who is not eligible for Christian salvation was not made by Jesus when He died on the cross; it was made by God the Father when He created the world ages ago and wrote the names of His elect in His Book of Life. Jesus simply died so that all whose names are included in the Book of Life could be given a chance to receive salvation by declaring their faith in Him and yielding their lives to Him.

Biblical Examples of Tares

Assuming the interpretation of this parable that has been provided thus far is correct, then there should be some examples of tares recorded in the Bible. The scriptures do provide us with a few such examples, the first of which is found in Genesis 6:1-7. Here we find that the "sons of God" (assumed to be disobedient angels) cohabited with the "daughters of men" and their children were called the "giants" (in Hebrew, *Nephilim* or *Rephaim*). Since this text states that these acts of cohabitation were displeasing to God, then it is clear that they were not a part of His original plan for the human race. Therefore we may conclude that this race of giants and their descendants would not have their names written in His Book of Life and can therefore be classified as human "tares."

Now since the great flood at the time of Noah presumably destroyed all of these giants and their descendants that were on earth at that time, we might conclude that all of these children of the devil were eliminated. However, if the procreation of a race of giants (*Nephilim*) was possible before the flood, then it seems reasonable to assume that the process might have been repeated after the flood, leading to the procreation of another group of non-elect human tares in the world today. This conclusion is supported in Numbers 13:33, in which the twelve Hebrew spies reported finding such giants later in the land of Canaan.

The actual method by which Satan's children came to be on the earth has been discussed to a limited extent in an earlier paragraph of this article. However, we do not have to understand the specific way in which such persons were placed on earth; for Jesus definitely stated that they are present among the children of God's kingdom (Matthew 13:38-39), and we must accept this as the truth. Jesus affirmed the existence of such persons again when He said to His disciples: *"Every plant which My heavenly Father did not plant shall be rooted up. Let them alone; they are blind guides of the blind. And if a blind man guides a blind man, both will fall into a pit." (Matthew 15:13-14)*

Here Jesus warned His disciples to leave the non-elect "tares" alone and not to waste their time in trying to lead them into salvation; and we should also be mindful of this advice as we attempt to evangelize the world today. God's gift of the discernment of spirits (see 1 Corinthians 12:10) is an indispensable tool for identifying the children of the devil.

Another scriptural example of persons identified by Jesus as sons of the devil is given in John 8:31-47. Jesus, using His gift of the discernment of spirits, identified the specific group of Pharisees being confronted in this passage as such. One other example of a tare mentioned in scripture is Judas Iscariot, who was identified in John 17:12 as the "son of perdition," i.e., the son of hell (see also John 6:70-71). This same title was given to the final Antichrist by Paul in 2 Thessalonians 2:3, for as we might expect, he will truly be a son of the devil. According to Matthew 13:40-42, the tares will be burned at the close of the age, for they are outside of God's saving grace.

Because those who have their names listed in the Book of Life have met the initial requirement for salvation, it seems reasonable that God will give them at least one opportunity to satisfy the remaining requirements. This is in agreement with the doctrine of predestination (or election) outlined by Paul in Romans 8:29-30, which reads: *"For whom He foreknew* [by writing their names in His Book of Life], *He predestined to become conformed to the image of His Son* [through spiritual rebirth], *that He* [Christ] *might be the first-born among many brethren; and whom He predestined, these He also called* [invited into His kingdom]; *and whom He called, these He also justified* [reckoned to be righteous]; *and whom He justified, these He also glorified* [transformed into new persons]."

Even though this passage from Romans 8 states that God will call His elect at some time during their lifetimes on earth, they are still free to accept or reject His invitation when it comes, for God does not want His kingdom to be inhabited by robots. Prior to the time of Christ, the children of Israel were called into righteousness by their priests and prophets (see Ezekiel 18:30-32). From Chapters 15 and 16 of 1 Samuel we see that King Saul rejected his call to obedience and righteousness, and God subsequently rejected him (see 1 Samuel 15:10-11, 26; 16:14).

Then in Matthew 19:16-22 we read the story of the rich man who rejected a call to righteous living given by Jesus. For Christians, this call comes when God gives them the faith for salvation (see John 6:44, 65; Ephesians 2:8-9), and this faith is a gift of grace, which of course is extended only to God's elect. It is also comforting to note from John 6:39 that Jesus does not intend to lose any of those whom God has given Him, i.e., those who have heard and accepted their call from God. Members of the elect group should be diligent to accept their divine invitation when it is offered in order to avoid the fate of the non-elect members of society (see Luke 14:16-20,24).

Summary and Conclusions

The previous discussion can be summarized as follows:

1. Jesus gave us the parable of the tares in the wheat field to explain the relationship between two groups of people on this earth today – the tares (the "sons of the evil one") and the wheat plants (the "sons of the kingdom").

2. Jesus gave His disciples a detailed interpretation of this parable; He interpreted it as an allegory, in which there was a direct relationship between each item of the parable and its counterpart in the spiritual kingdom of heaven.

3. Just as tares (or weeds) can never become wheat plants in real life, "sons of the evil one" can never become "sons of the kingdom" in spiritual life. Therefore, the former group can never be eligible for God's salvation.

4. God the Father planned the existence of every one of His elect children at the time of creation, and He recorded their names in His Book of Life at that time. This fulfilled one (but not all) of the conditions necessary for their salvation.

5. The fact that God planned the births of His elect at the time of creation implies that He also planned the marriages of their parents and the conception of their elect children.

In each case, if either of these two events does not take place as planned, then the name of the unborn child will not be found in the Book of Life. Furthermore, there is no way in which any other name can be added subsequently to His Book of Life.

6. Before one of God's elect can become one of His children and enter the kingdom of God, he or she must be drawn to Jesus by God the Father and be given the gift of faith for salvation. This is the second step in the Christian salvation experience.

7. As the third and final condition for Christian salvation, the person must accept his or her invitation to be born of the Spirit and enter the kingdom of God. At this time a new living spirit will be created within the person and for the first time he or she can be called a true child of God.

8. Entries into God's Book of Life are not limited to the names of Christians; the names of other righteous persons (primarily Jews) are also included. Anyone who is destined to become a resident of either the new heaven (the New Jerusalem) or the new earth must have his or her name written in the Book of Life.

9. The Bible contains a few examples of human tares (sons of the evil one), such as the giants (*Nephilim*) of Genesis 6:1-7, Judas Iscariot (John 6:70-71; 17:12), and also a particular group of Jews confronted by Jesus in John 8:31-47.

10. Jesus cautioned His disciples not to waste their time trying to convert those recognized as human "tares," for they cannot be converted into Christians (see Matthew 15:13-14). In a certain sense, they can be considered to be Satan's decoys, placed here to waste the time of Christian evangelists.

As I stated at the beginning of this article, I realize the interpretation that has been given for this parable will be difficult for some to accept. Consequently, I asked God once again whether or not this explanatory document is really necessary, and He assured me that many evangelists need to understand its contents. It will give comfort to many evangelists who have been unsuccessful in trying to lead human tares into Christianity, and it will prevent others from wasting their time in trying to convert unconvertible persons. It will also provide further insight concerning the true nature of God and His overall plan for our salvation.

So I have been obedient, and I have tried faithfully to present explanations and interpretations that God has given to me. I pray that He will let my words have real meaning to the readers of this book, and that He will make His truths acceptable to everyone who desires to know the true meaning of this parable.

E. "Berk" Hammond

THE HARLOT
CALLED "BABYLON"
(First released in August 2009)

*   *   *   *   *   *   *

The first six verses of Rev. 17 introduce a harlot called "Babylon," riding on a beast having seven heads and ten horns. These verses read as follows:

> *(1) Then one of the seven angels who had the seven bowls came and talked with me, saying to me, "Come, I will show you the judgment of the great harlot who sits on many waters,*
> *(2) with whom the kings of the earth committed fornication, and the inhabitants of the earth were made drunk with the wine of her fornication."*
> *(3) So he carried me away in the Spirit into the wilderness. And I saw a woman sitting on a scarlet beast which was full of names of blasphemy, having seven heads and ten horns.*
> *(4) The woman was arrayed in purple and scarlet, and adorned with gold and precious stones and pearls, having in her hand a golden cup full of abominations and the filthiness of her fornication.*

> *(5) And on her forehead a name was written: MYSTERY,*
> *BABYLON THE GREAT, THE MOTHER OF*
> *HARLOTS AND OF THE ABOMINATIONS OF*
> *THE EARTH.*
> *(6) I saw the woman, drunk with the blood of the saints*
> *and with the blood of the martyrs of Jesus. And when I*
> *saw her, I marveled with great amazement.*

From the descriptions given in Rev. 13:1-10 and Rev. 17:8 it seems obvious that the beast with seven heads and ten horns on which the harlot is mounted represents the Antichrist. He will come to earth from the "bottomless pit," according to Rev. 17:8. However, there has been much speculation concerning the identity of his harlot passenger. The Internet's Wikipedia lists the following nine organizations or groups as possible candidates to be represented by this harlot:

1.   Rome and the Roman Empire

2.   Earthly Jerusalem

3.   The Roman Catholic church

4.   The Protestant Reformation

5.   Traditionalist Catholics

6.   Swedenborgianism

7.   The Latter Day Saint movement

8.   The Soviet Union

9.   Jehovah's Witnesses

At one time this list also included a tenth group, the Muslim worshippers of Allah. However, this group has been removed, probably due to many Muslim protests. The Wikipedia article also lists the reasons that have been given for considering each of the nine candidates listed.

Considering the large number of possible candidates that have been suggested, it seems obvious that there is no real knowledge concerning the identity of this harlot. The purpose of this paper is to investigate Bible scriptures that provide useful information concerning the harlot's identity in an effort to determine who or what she represents.

One significant fact is that she comes into the picture riding on a beast representing the Antichrist. This seems to imply that she did not exist before the arrival of the Antichrist. Therefore, she must represent a group or an organization to be founded by the Antichrist subsequent to his arrival. If this is so, then none of the candidates listed above should be considered.

There are two verses of scripture, Rev. 17:6 and 18:24, that indicate this harlot is responsible for *"the blood of the prophets and saints, and of all who were slain on the earth."* This statement may sound as if it might apply to all prophets and saints, including those who lived before the arrival of the Antichrist, but it is my opinion that it applies only to those who will live under the rule of the Antichrist.

Another clue concerning her identity is given in Rev. 18:7, which reads as follows: *"In the measure that she glorified herself and lived luxuriously, in the same measure give her torment and sorrow; for she says in her heart, 'I sit as queen, and am no widow, and will not see sorrow.'"* From this it is apparent that she considers herself to be a queen, with a living husband. Since she was brought into the picture riding on the beast that represents the Antichrist, then it seems obvious that her husband would be the Antichrist, and she will be his wife. She and her activities are also described in Isaiah 47:5 where she is called a *"daughter of the Chaldeans"* (from the land of Chaldea, or Mesopotamia). This indicates that she will be in some way related to the nations of the Middle East.

Since the wife of Christ Jesus will be the Christian church, and since the Antichrist will try to duplicate everything that Christ Jesus plans to do, then it seems that his harlot wife should also be some type of church organization. In Rev. 18:4 God tells His people: *"Come out of her, my people, lest you share in her sins, and lest you receive of her plagues."* From this it is obvious that this harlot church organization will at some time include some of God's elect. It is likely to be a very large organization, and since the Christian church did not exist before Jesus' ministry began on this earth, then it is not likely that this new apostate church will be formed before the arrival of the Antichrist.

There is another passage of scripture that tends to support these ideas. This scripture is found in Zech. 5:5-11, and it reads as follows:

(5) Then the angel who talked with me came out and said to me, "Lift your eyes now, and see what this is that goes forth."

(6) So I asked, "What is it?" And he said, "It is a basket that is going forth." He also said, "This is their resemblance throughout the earth:
(7) Here is a lead disc lifted up, and this is a woman sitting inside the basket";
(8) then he said, "This is Wickedness!" And he thrust her down into the basket, and threw the lead cover over its mouth.
(9) Then I raised my eyes and looked, and there were two women, coming with the wind in their wings; for they had wings like the wings of a stork, and they lifted up the basket between earth and heaven.
(10) So I said to the angel who talked with me, "Where are they carrying the basket?"
(11) And he said to me, "To build a house for it in the land of Shinar; when it is ready, the basket will be set there on its base."

This passage tells of a wicked woman who is being taken to the "land of Shinar" (Mesopotamia), where a house (apparently her headquarters) will be built for her. It is quite likely that the woman being carried in the basket is in fact the harlot introduced in Rev. 17, therefore it seems reasonable to assume that the apostate church, to be called the wife of the Antichrist, will have its headquarters in Mesopotamia.

The passage also states that the basket in which she is carried will be set on its base in the house which is to be built. Obviously this basket must symbolize something, but what could it be? It is quite possible that the basket symbolizes a new Bible, which would be the foundation of the new church, just as the holy Bible is the foundation of the Christian church, and the Koran is the foundation of the Islamic church. This new Bible could be set on its base (or pedestal) within the church headquarters building.

As for the city in Mesopotamia that will be the headquarters for this apostate church, Rev. 17:9 provides a clue concerning its identity. This verse reads as follows: *"Here is the mind which has wisdom: The seven heads are seven mountains on which the woman sits."* Apparently this city will be located on seven mountains (or hills), and of course the most famous city on seven hills is Rome, Italy. However, there are other cities that claim to be built on seven hills, and since Rome is not located in Mesopotamia, it should not be considered.

Now this apostate church, which is referred to as "Babylon" in the Revelation, will eventually be completely destroyed by the Antichrist and the ten nations under his control. The verses that tell of her destruction also provide additional information concerning her identity. These verses, Rev. 18:9-10 and 17-18, read as follows:

> *(9) The kings of the earth who committed fornication and lived luxuriously with her will weep and lament for her, when they see the smoke of her burning,*
> *(10) standing at a distance for fear of her torment, saying, "Alas, alas, that great city Babylon, that mighty city! For in one hour your judgment has come."*
>
> -----
>
> *(17) For in one hour such great riches came to nothing. Every shipmaster, all who travel by ship, sailors, and as many as trade on the sea, stood at a distance*
> *(18) and cried out when they saw the smoke of her burning, saying, "What is like this great city?"*

From these verses three things become apparent: (1) the city will be destroyed in one hour, (2) no one is able to come near the city after it has been destroyed, and (3) the city is apparently a seaport.

Verse 17 specifically mentions shipmasters, sailors and those who trade by the sea as being primarily effected by the destruction of this city. Thus it seems safe to conclude that the city will be a seaport, and that a nuclear bomb will destroy it. Only a nuclear bomb would be able to destroy the city in just one hour, and also keep everyone away subsequently due to nuclear radiation.

Of all of the seaport cities in Mesopotamia that are situated on seven hills, only one is predominant – Istanbul, Turkey (formerly called Constantinople). The Internet Wikipedia recognizes this city as being built on seven hills, and it is located near the sea. Wikipedia also lists Istanbul as one of the seaport cities on the sea of Marmara.

Conclusions

The foregoing analysis leads to the following conclusions:

1. The harlot called "Babylon" apparently represents the wife of the Antichrist – a new apostate church.

2. This apostate church does not exist at the present time. It is expected that it will be formed after the Antichrist arrives.

3. The headquarters for this new church is likely to be located in the city of Istanbul, Turkey.

4. Initially, this new church will have some of God's elect as its members, but they are warned by God to come out of her in order to avoid receiving her plagues.

5. The Antichrist and his ten subordinate nations, using one or more nuclear bombs, will eventually destroy this new church and the city in which she is located.

I trust that the facts that have been presented here will have some real meaning for those who read this document. At least it might serve to stop the false identification of existing organizations as candidates for the "harlot of Babylon."

E. "Berk" Hammond

THE 144,000 HEBREW SERVANTS OF GOD

(First released in February 2009)

* * * * * * *

The text of Rev. 7:1-8 deals with the selection and sealing of 144,000 Jewish servants of God who are to be assigned special duties later by Christ Jesus. This passage indicates that 12,000 servants will be taken from each of twelve tribes of Israel. The purpose of this article is to examine the passages of scripture that relate to this particular group of God's servants in an to attempt to determine the way in which they fit into the overall end-time scenario.

This group of Jewish servants is mentioned only two times in the Book of Revelation – in Rev. 7:1-8 and in Rev. 14:1-5. The first of these two passages describes the way in which they will be selected and sealed, and the second passage enlarges their description and portrays them in heaven singing songs as a heavenly choir. Therefore it is reasonable to conclude that they will be taken into heaven via some type of rapture event following their being selected and sealed for service.

These servants of God are introduced in the first three verses of Rev. 7, which read as follows:

(1) After these things I saw four angels standing at the four corners of the earth, holding the four winds of the

earth, that the wind should not blow on the earth, on the sea, or on any tree.

(2) Then I saw another angel ascending from the east, having the seal of the living God. And he cried with a loud voice to the four angels to whom it was granted to harm the earth and the sea,

(3) saying, "Do not harm the earth, the sea, or the trees till we have <u>sealed the servants of our God</u> on their foreheads."

These verses introduce the four angels who have full power to harm the earth, the sea, and the trees during the coming tribulation period. They are told not to harm the earth, the sea, or the trees until the selection and sealing of the 144,000 servants has been completed. According to Rev. 8:7, the first event of the tribulation period will be the burning of one-third of all the trees and all the green grass on earth. Therefore, it may be concluded that the selection and sealing of the 144,000 servants of God will be a pre-tribulational process.

The next five verses in this chapter (Rev. 7:4-8) describe the process by which these servants will be selected – 12,000 servants will be taken from each of the twelve tribes of Israel. However, the names of the tribes listed here are not quite the same as those listed in Num. 1:5-15 or 1:20-43.

Ten of the twelve tribes listed in the Revelation are identical with those listed in Numbers, but note that the tribe of Joseph has replaced the tribe of his son Ephraim, and the priestly tribe of Levi has replaced the tribe of Dan. We may wonder why these two replacements were necessary, but the most likely reason is found in the text of 1 Kings 12:28-30. From this passage we see that Jeroboam, King of Israel, made two golden calves for the citizens of Israel to worship, and he placed one in Bethel (considered to be in the tribal region of Ephraim) and the other in the region of Dan.

God considered these idols to be a great source of sin for Israel, and He apparently does not want any members of these two tribes to be included in the group of 144,000 Jewish servants to be brought before His throne. Therefore He must have replaced Ephraim's name with the name of his father Joseph, and Dan's name with the name of Levi, the head of the tribe of priests that was not included in the original list of the twelve tribes of Israel.

The first five verses of Rev. 14 provide more information concerning the 144,000 servants of God. These verses read as follows:

(1) Then I looked, and behold, a Lamb standing on Mount Zion, and with Him one hundred and forty-four thousand, having His Father's name written on their foreheads.

(2) And I heard a voice from heaven, like the voice of many waters, and like the voice of loud thunder. And I heard the sound of harpists playing their harps.

(3) They sang as it were a new song before the throne, before the four living creatures, and the elders; and no one could learn that song except the hundred and forty-four thousand who were redeemed from the earth.

(4) These are the ones who were not defiled with women, for they are virgins. These are the ones who follow the Lamb wherever He goes. These were redeemed from among men, being first fruits to God and to the Lamb.

(5) And in their mouth was found no deceit, for they are without fault before the throne of God.

Verse 1 above indicates that although these servants have God's name written on their foreheads, they apparently will look to Jesus for leadership and direction. This seems to indicate that these servants will probably be a gift from God to His Son, perhaps a wedding gift. The loud voice coming from heaven (in Verse 2) must be the voice of God, possibly presenting His gift of 144,000 servants to Jesus. From Verse 3 it is apparent that one of their missions will be to sing songs as a heavenly choir, and the particular song is one that is known only by them. It is my opinion that they may also be directed to serve the Christians as singing waiters at Christ's great marriage supper.

From Verses 4-5 it can be seen that these servants will all be celibate men who have had no relations with women. Also, they have not practiced any deceit and are said to be without fault before the throne of God. But as we shall see in a later section of this document, their level of purity is likely to be the result of their being cleansed with divine fire from heaven. God gives only the very best of everything to His Son.

It has been shown that the 144,000 servants of God will be selected and sealed before the tribulation begins. However, the only events that are described in the Revelation just before the sounding of the first tribulational trumpet are those found in Rev. 8:3-5. These verses describe (1) the effects of God's visit to the earth in response to the prayers of the saints, and (2) the casting of coals of divine fire over the earth (the baptism with fire). In order to understand the way in which this passage of scripture relates to the 144,000 Hebrew servants of God, another Biblical description of this event must be found.

Since God called Ezekiel to present His messages to the nation Israel (see Ezek. 2:2-4), we might expect to find some prophecy in his book relating to the 144,000 servants of God described in the Revelation. There is a passage in Ezekiel, Chapters 8-10, that seems to have a bearing on the selection and sealing of these servants of God. Although this entire passage is worth reading, for the sake of brevity I will not print it here in its entirety. Instead, only the pertinent verses will be quoted.

In Chapter 8, God showed Ezekiel the many different ways in which the citizens of Israel are living sinful lives, and in the last verse God promised to punish them for their deeds and to reject their future pleas for help. Then the story continues in Chapter 9, the first four verses of which read as follows:

> *(1) Then He called out in my hearing with a loud voice, saying, "Let those who have charge over the city draw near, each with a deadly weapon in his hand."*
> *(2) And suddenly six men came from the direction of the upper gate, which faces north, each with his battle-ax in his hand. One man among them was clothed with linen and had a writer's inkhorn at his side. They went in and stood beside the bronze altar.*
> *(3) Now the glory of the God of Israel had gone up from the cherub, where it had been, to the threshold of the temple. And He called to the man clothed with linen, who had the writer's inkhorn at his side;*
> *(4) and the Lord said to him, "Go through the midst of the city, through the midst of Jerusalem, and put a mark on the foreheads of the men who sigh and cry over all the abominations that are done within it."*

This passage shows God preparing his warrior angels to destroy the sinful inhabitants of the city (Jerusalem). However, before their destruction begins He directs a "man clothed with linen" to go through the city and place a mark on the foreheads of all the righteous men that he can find.

It seems reasonable to assume that this command is directly comparable to the command given to the four angels in Rev. 7:3 saying: *"Do not harm the earth, the sea, or the trees till we have sealed the servants of our God on their foreheads."* Therefore we may conclude that this selection and marking of God's 144,000 servants will take place in a time of impending disaster for the nation Israel. Finally, Verse 11 states that the "man clothed with linen" returned and announced: *"I have done as You commanded me."*

There is some additional information to be gained from Chapter 10. Verses 1-2 read as follows:

> *(1) And I looked, and there in the firmament that was above the head of the cherubim, there appeared something like a sapphire stone, having the appearance of the likeness of a throne.*
> *(2) Then He spoke to the man clothed with linen, and said, "Go in among the wheels, under the cherub, fill your hands with coals of fire from among the cherubim, and scatter them over the city." And he went in as I watched.*

In Verse 2 the "man clothed with linen" is told to take divine coals of fire and scatter them over the city. Then Verses 6-7 show the man's obedience to this command as follows:

> *(6) Then it happened, when He commanded the man clothed in linen, saying, "Take fire from among the wheels, from among the cherubim," that he went in and stood beside the wheels.*
> *(7) And the cherub stretched out his hand from among the cherubim to the fire that was among the cherubim, and took some of it and put it into the hands of the man clothed with linen, who took it and went out.*

This last verse does not state what the "man clothed with linen" did with the fire when he went out, but it is assumed that he scattered it over the city as he was told to do in Verse 2. This scattering of fire is similar to that which is to be accomplished by an angel in Rev. 8:5, and it seems reasonable to assume that these two scatterings of fire might be one and the same event. If they are the same, then the fire would be distributed only to the 144,000 Jews who had received the mark on their foreheads and to those Christians chosen to be rulers under Christ Jesus during the Millennium and thereafter. This event will be the baptism with fire.

The marking and sealing of the 144,000 Hebrew servants is not portrayed in the apocalyptic section of the Revelation to John, probably because it is to be conducted in secret, and also because it is not related in any way to the Christian church. However, if a description of this event were to be inserted into the apocalyptic section, it should be entered somewhere between Rev. 8:2 and Rev. 8:5.

In my earlier document entitled "Closing Events of the Church Age" this scattering of fire by the angel in Rev. 8:5 was called the "baptism with fire," just as it was predicted by John the Baptist. Its purpose will be to prepare the ruling Christians to be rulers under Christ Jesus during the Millennium, and in a similar manner the 144,000 servants of God also will probably be baptized with fire to prepare them to be servants of Christ during the Millennium and thereafter. After all, they will be present on earth when this baptism takes place, and it is quite logical to assume that they will be included in it.

Comments Concerning the Timing of Their Rapture

The Bible does not seem to give any specific indication of the time at which these servants of God will be translated into heaven, and neither does it describe any mission that they might have on earth prior to their being taken to heaven. It is my opinion that these servants of God will be taken off the earth, together with the "chosen" Christians, in the partial rapture. However, while the Christians will be sent back to earth to carry out their post-resurrection ministries, the 144,000 Jewish servants will obviously remain in heaven to perform their assigned duties there.

The first six verses of Rev. 12 tell of a future event that could be interpreted to be the rapture of the 144,000 servants of God:

(1) Now a great sign appeared in heaven: a woman clothed with the sun, with the moon under her feet, and on her head a garland of twelve stars.

(2) Then being with child, she cried out in labor and in pain to give birth.

(3) And another sign appeared in heaven: behold, a great, fiery red dragon having seven heads and ten horns, and seven diadems on his heads.

(4) His tail drew a third of the stars of heaven and threw them to the earth. And the dragon stood before the woman who was ready to give birth, to devour her Child as soon as it was born.

(5) She bore a male Child who was to rule all nations with a rod of iron. And <u>her Child was caught up to God and His throne</u>.

(6) Then the woman fled into the wilderness, where she has a place prepared by God, that they should feed her there one thousand two hundred and sixty days.

The woman mentioned in Verse 1 is generally considered to represent the nation Israel, and this passage of scripture has often been interpreted to apply to the birth of Christ Jesus. However, Verse 5 doesn't seem to fit that event very well. It implies that her "male Child" was taken up to God and His throne shortly after being born, and that did not happen following Jesus' birth. Jesus remained on earth for around 33 years before departing for heaven. It seems more likely that her "male Child" should be interpreted collectively to mean the 144,000 male servants of God rather than Christ Jesus. It is expected that they will be taken up to heaven via the partial rapture shortly after they are selected and given seals on their foreheads.

Verse 5 also states that this "male Child" will rule the nations with a rod of iron – an action normally attributed to Jesus (see Rev, 2:27; 19:15). However, this statement could also apply to the 144,000 servants of Jesus who are likely to become soldiers in His army during the Millennium and be directed to execute His commands.

Summary and Conclusions

From a comparison of Rev. 7:1-8, Rev. 14:1-5, Ezek. Chas. 8-10 and Rev. 8:3-5 the following conclusions seem to be appropriate:

1. Prior to the start of the tribulation period, 144,000 Israeli men will be selected and sealed to be servants of Christ during the Millennium and thereafter. 12,000 servants will be taken from each of twelve tribes of Israel. It is likely that God the Father will present them to Christ Jesus as a wedding present prior to the "marriage supper of the Lamb."

2. At some time following their selection these servants of God will be translated into heaven (probably via the partial rapture) where they will become servants of Christ. One of their initial duties will be to serve as a heavenly choir, singing beautiful songs for the residents of heaven. Later they will probably be assigned as soldiers in Christ's army to assist Him in maintaining order on the earth during the Millennium.

3. There is no specific indication of the time at which their transfer to heaven will take place, but there are reasons to believe that they may be taken with the ruling Christians in the partial rapture.

4. These servants will probably be baptized with fire, just as the ruling Christians will be, prior to the start of the tribulation period. This would qualify them to be servants of Christ during the Millennium and thereafter.

5. These Hebrew servants will all be celibate men in whom no fault or deceit can be found. It is likely that their purity will be the result of their having been baptized with fire.

Both the purpose and the mission of the 144,000 servants of God have been described by Christian leaders in different ways, but I trust that this paper will serve to shed more light on these topics. I pray that the Holy Spirit will lead those who read it into the truth and to a better understanding of this interesting subject.

E. "Berk" Hammond

THE MARRIAGE SUPPER OF THE LAMB
(First released in November 1987)

* * * * * * *

Contents

- Introduction
- The Divine Marriage Ceremony
- Transportation to the Divine Marriage Supper
- The Destiny of the Raptured Christians
- Summary and Concluding Remarks

* * * * * * *

Introduction

There is an event described in the Revelation to John in which all true Christians desire to participate; it will be the climax of all Christian experiences. It is the "marriage supper of the Lamb," found in Rev. 19:1-10.

The primary purpose of this exegesis is to:

1. Highlight this future celebration as it is described in the Bible.

2. Interpret those Biblical passages that illustrate the way in which selected Christians will be assembled to take part in it.

3. Outline the eventual destiny of those Christians who are allowed to participate in this marriage ceremony.

This is not an evangelistic document intended to persuade non-Christians to accept the Christian faith. It is an analysis of those Biblical texts that relate to this divine marriage ceremony with the objective of providing a clear and coherent pattern for the events that both precede and follow this glorious future event.

The Divine Marriage Ceremony

The first six verses of Rev. 19 portray the exalted worship scene in heaven that will set the stage for this divine wedding celebration. Since the word "Hallelujah" is used four times in these six verses, this has been labeled the "fourfold Hallelujah passage." It describes a future scene in which every citizen of heaven will be completely and totally devoted to the act of praising God for His mighty works and for judging and destroying the "great harlot" – the apostate church of the Antichrist. The destruction of this harlot, called "Babylon," is described in Rev.17:14-18.

Verses 7-10 of Rev. 19 are listed below. They describe the divine marriage ceremony – the event in which Christ Jesus, His church bride, and His church body will be permanently united.

> *(7) Let us be glad and rejoice and give Him glory, for the marriage of the Lamb has come, and His wife has made herself ready.*
> *(8) And to her it was granted to be arrayed in fine linen, clean and bright, for the fine linen is the righteous acts of the saints.*
> *(9) Then he said to me, "Write: 'Blessed are those who are called to the marriage supper of the Lamb!'" And he said to me, "These are the true sayings of God."*

(10) And I fell at his feet to worship him. But he said to me, "See that you do not do that! I am your fellow servant, and of your brethren who have the testimony of Jesus. Worship God! For the testimony of Jesus is the spirit of prophecy."

In Verse 9 of this scripture text the angel makes it clear that those who attend this glorious marriage ceremony will do so by invitation only, and that those who accept their invitations will be blessed immeasurably. His declaration implies that others may be invited to witness this event in addition to the bride, the bridegroom (Christ Jesus), and the angels of heaven. Therefore it is appropriate to identify each of the Christian groups that will be ushered into this magnificent celebration and to determine what a person must do to have his or her name placed on the invitation list.

The New Testament contains several references to both the body and the bride of Christ. For example, 1 Cor. 12:27, Eph. 4:12, and Col. 1:18 refer to the church as the body of Christ, while in Rev. 19:7 and 21:9 the church is called the bride and the wife of Christ. Obviously these terms are mutually exclusive, for it is impossible for the church to be the bride (or the wife) and the body of the bridegroom simultaneously. This leads to the conclusion that before the marriage ceremony begins, the Christian saints will be divided into at least two groups – the body of Christ and the bride of Christ.

The separation of a special group of Christian souls is foretold in Rev. 6:9. This verse portrays the souls of the dead Christians who have died as Christian martyrs, resting in paradise and isolated from the souls of other Christians. They are shown to be segregated as a special group under the altar of the temple in heaven. This suggests that the Christian martyrs may constitute the true bride of Christ, being held together as a group under the altar, waiting to be joined by other martyred Christians before participating in the divine marriage ceremony.

Such a group of Christian martyrs would logically be entitled to be Christ's special bride because they will have made the supreme sacrifice by giving their lives for Him, just as He gave His life for them and for others on the cross. Other "chosen" Christian saints who are not destined to die as martyrs must therefore constitute the body of Christ.

Paul made this clear to the Corinthian church in 1 Cor. 12:27 when he said: *"Now you are the body of Christ, and members individually."*

Considering these facts, it is obvious why the writers of the New Testament epistles called the church the body of Christ prior to the divine marriage ceremony in heaven. After all, it would have been impossible for the writers of the New Testament epistles to know if any particular Christian was destined to die a martyr's death while the person was still alive.

Consequently, the living Christians about whom the New Testament epistles were written could only have been regarded as members of the body of Christ, responsible for following His directions and carrying out His commandments during their lives on earth. Their qualifications for being members of the bride of Christ could not be determined until the time of their death – that is, did they or did they not die as Christian martyrs? However, Jesus reminded us of God's law governing marriage when He said:

> *(6)* But from the beginning of the creation, God *made them male and female.*
> *(7) For this reason a man shall leave his father and mother and be joined to his wife,*
> *(8) and the two shall become one flesh;* so then they are no longer two, but one flesh.
> *(9)* Therefore what God has joined together, let not man separate. (Mark 10:6-9)

Of course it is only logical that God's rules that govern a marriage for the citizens of earth must also apply to the divine marriage ceremony in heaven, for God's laws are universal. Therefore, once the marriage between Christ Jesus and His bride takes place in heaven, then in accordance with God's law Christ Jesus' body and His bride will become inseparable and indistinguishable – they will become "one flesh." From that time on they will be a unified group, called *"the bride, the wife of the Lamb"* (see Rev. 21:9).

Thus far only the Christians that constitute the bride and the body of Christ have been considered, but there may be other Christians in attendance. In another of my articles titled "Closing Events of the Church Age," it was shown that there are two different types of

Christians on the earth today – (1) Christians who have been chosen to be rulers under Christ during the Millennium, and (2) Christians who have been called to be servants in God's heavenly temple after their physical deaths. It is obvious that Christians constituting the bride and the body of Christ would have to be those chosen to be rulers under Christ, but what about the Christians who have been called to be servants in God's temple?

Remember that in Rev. 19:9 the angel is quoted as saying: *"Write: 'Blessed are those who are called to the marriage supper of the Lamb!'"* It is my belief that the called Christians will be invited to attend the divine marriage ceremony as guests of the bridegroom, Christ Jesus. Thus the three groups of Christians attending the marriage ceremony would be the bride, the body, and the guests of the bridegroom, Christ Jesus.

There is little more to be said about the details of the marriage ceremony itself. This event was mentioned figuratively by Jesus in His parables of the marriage feast (Matt. 22:1-14), the great dinner (Luke 14:16-24), and the ten virgins (Matt. 25:1-13). However, the passage in Rev. 19:1-10 provides the only Biblical source of information concerning the actual details of the marriage celebration, and these details are quite limited.

Needless to say, this event will be of paramount importance to all Christians, and this prompted the angel to repeat to John the words of God in Verse 9: *"Blessed are those who are called to the marriage supper of the Lamb."* It will now be of interest to determine the way in which the Christian participants will be selected and taken to this glorious marriage celebration, and also the roles that they can expect to fill thereafter.

Transportation to the Divine Marriage Supper

Of course, any eligible Christians who died physically prior to the divine marriage ceremony would be living in heaven (or Paradise) in their spiritual bodies and would only have to be taken to the site designated for the marriage ceremony. But what will happen to the Christians who are alive on earth at the time that the wedding ceremony is being initiated? How will they be brought into heaven in time for the ceremony?

It seems reasonable to assume that the divine marriage will not take place until all eligible Christians have been taken from earth to heaven and all evangelistic work on earth has ceased. Otherwise, the last Christians to be converted would miss this grand and glorious wedding event.

The final gathering of the Christian saints at the close of the church age is described by Paul in 1 Thess. 4:13-18 and in 1 Cor. 15:51-53. This event is commonly called the rapture of the saints, although the word "rapture" is not to be found in the Bible. The word *"raptos"* was used in 1 Thess. 4:17 in the Latin Vulgate Edition of the Bible to describe the catching up process to be experienced in the rapture, and it is from this Latin word *"raptos"* that our English word "rapture" is derived.

Briefly, the rapture event can be simply defined as the process by which all eligible living Christians will be taken supernaturally to a place within the earth's atmosphere where they will meet with Christ Jesus for the first time. Then they will receive their imperishable spiritual bodies and be translated to heaven to attend the divine marriage ceremony. This rapture event is described in Rev. 14:14-16:

> *(14) Then I looked, and behold, a white cloud, and on the cloud sat One like the Son of Man, having on His head a golden crown, and in His hand a sharp sickle.*
> *(15) And another angel came out of the temple, crying with a loud voice to Him who sat on the cloud, "Thrust in Your sickle and reap, for the time has come for You to reap, for the harvest of the earth is ripe."*
> *(16) So He who sat on the cloud thrust in His sickle on the earth, and the earth was reaped.*

Note that in this passage there is no mention of any judgment; **all** of the wheat plants (representing true Christians) are taken from the earth. Note also that the description of this event in the Revelation follows the sounding of the seventh and last tribulational trumpet in Rev. 11:15, just as Paul said that it would in 1 Cor. 15:51-53. Since this rapture event is pictured as a harvesting operation, it has been called the "harvest" rapture.

Now that God's plan for selecting and transporting the eligible Christians to the divine marriage ceremony has been found, let us look at the events that are to follow this marriage celebration.

The Destiny of the Raptured Christians

It has been shown that two different types of Christians will be attending the marriage ceremony: (1) those chosen to be rulers under Christ during the Millennium, and (2) those called to be servants of God in His heavenly temple. At the completion of the marriage ceremony, the called Christians can be taken directly to God's heavenly temple to begin their acts of service there, and the destiny of the chosen Christians will now be considered.

The first major event to follow the marriage ceremony will be the battle of Armageddon, in which Christ and His armies will fight and defeat the armies of the Antichrist and cast him and his false prophet into the lake of fire (see Rev. 19:20). As for Satan, he will be bound with chains and cast into the bottomless pit, where he will remain for 1,000 years, until the end of the Millennium (see Rev. 20:1-3).

Verse 4 of Rev. 20 is of particular interest at this point because it describes the establishment of Christ's millennial kingdom on earth following the battle of Armageddon:

> *(4) And I saw thrones, and they sat on them, and judgment was committed to them. Then I saw the souls of those who had been beheaded for their witness to Jesus and for the word of God, who had not worshiped the beast or his image, and had not received his mark on their foreheads or on their hands. And they lived and reigned with Christ for a thousand years.*

This verse identifies an assembly of judges and rulers under Christ – Christians who have devoted their lives to Jesus and to following the Word of God, remaining true to their faith in opposition to the Antichrist. Although the subordinate citizens of earth who were not included in the rapture are not mentioned specifically, they are included by implication, for those who are appointed judges and rulers could not fill their assigned roles if there were no subjects to be judged and governed.

Another distinction can be made between the ruling and the subordinate classes of people. The rulers will be brought to earth via the "first resurrection" (see Rev. 20:5), and they will have received spiritual bodies in accordance with Paul's declaration:

> *(42) So also is the resurrection of the dead. The body is sown in corruption, it is raised in incorruption. It is sown in dishonor, it is raised in glory.*
> *(43) It is sown in weakness, it is raised in power. (44) It is sown a natural body, it is raised a spiritual body. There is a natural body, and there is a spiritual body."*
> (1 Cor. 15:42-44)

This is also confirmed in Rev. 20:6, which states that they will rule with Christ for a thousand years – a period much longer than the normal human life span.

As for the subordinate citizens, note that in describing Christ's role during the Millennium, Paul said the last enemy of God to be abolished would be death (see 1 Cor. 15:26) and, according to Rev. 20:14, death will not be abolished until the end of the Millennium. Therefore, it is reasonable to assume that the subordinate citizens of the nations of earth will live normal physical lives during the Millennium, with new citizens being born and older persons dying periodically.

Note also that in Verse 4 above, the rulers are referred to as *"those who had been beheaded because of the testimony of Jesus and because of the Word of God."* A casual inspection of this verse might lead to the conclusion that it refers to the Christian martyrs; but a more extensive examination reveals that the word "beheaded," as it is used here, has a special symbolic meaning for which there is an explanation.

The Greek word *"pelekizo,"* which is used in this verse and translated as "beheaded," is a unique word that is used only once in the New Testament. The Greek word *"apokephalizo,"* derived from the word *"kephale"* (meaning "head"), is the usual word for decapitation; it is used four times in the New Testament in relation to the beheading of John the Baptist. The special word used in Rev. 20:4 is derived from *"pelekus"* (meaning "ax"), signifying the severing or separating of something with an ax (see W. E. Vine's *Expository Dictionary of New Testament Words*).

If Jesus had meant to imply physical decapitation when He gave this message to John, it is logical that He would have used the usual word *"apokephalizo."* But since He used the special word *"pelekizo,"* it is apparent that a symbolic death resulting from the forcible separation of some undesirable part of the human anatomy was implied in lieu of physical decapitation. Of course the head contains the brain – the center of a person's mind, will and emotions, and the control center for his self-centered actions and reactions. Thus if a person were to lose his head he would lose control of his body and would die, unless some new form of bodily control were substituted.

Such a substitution process was described by Paul in his letter to the Galatians when he said: *"I have been crucified with Christ; it is no longer I who live, but Christ lives in me; and the life which I now live in the flesh I live by faith in the Son of God, who loved me and gave Himself for me."* (Gal. 2:20) And to the Corinthians he wrote: *"Therefore, if anyone is in Christ, he is a new creation; old things have passed away; behold, all things have become new."* (2 Cor. 5:17).

Thus it is expected that a Christian will die to his old self (severing his self-will, symbolized by his head) and will yield control of his life to Christ and the Holy Spirit by being spiritually regenerated and baptized with the Holy Spirit. It seems logical that this act is implied by the special Greek word *"pelekizo,"* used in Rev. 20:4.

The assignment of ruling positions to Christians chosen to participate in the divine marriage ceremony is also supported by Luke's version of the parable of the talents (or "minas"), which describes the way in which the raptured Christians will be judged and rewarded. In this parable the man who received ten minas was told: *"Well done, good servant; because you were faithful in a very little thing, <u>have authority over ten cities</u>."* (Luke 19:17) Further confirmation was given by Jesus when He told His disciples that they would eventually become judges of the twelve tribes of Israel (see Matt. 19:28).

For additional confirmation regarding the destiny of Christians chosen to be judges and rulers in Christ's millennial government, remember Paul's declaration to the Corinthian church: *"Do you not know that <u>the saints will judge the world</u>? ... Do you not know that we shall judge angels?" (1 Cor. 6:2a, 3a)* Also, remember the promise that Jesus made to overcomers in the church of Thyatira when He said: *"To him who overcomes and does My will to the end, I will give authority over the nations – he will rule them with an iron scepter; he will dash them to pieces like pottery – just as I have received authority from My Father."* (Rev. 2:26-27 – NIV) Thus the scriptures make it quite clear that the raptured "overcomers" will be assigned ruling positions in the government of Christ Jesus during the Millennium.

Some persons may have imagined life during the Millennium as a time of peace and tranquility, but if the Christians are to rule with a "an iron scepter," the concept of an entirely peaceful government may be erroneous. In discussing this topic Paul said: *"For He [Christ] must reign until He has put all enemies under His feet. The last enemy that will be destroyed is death."* (1 Cor. 15:25-26) Then from Rev. 20:14 it is apparent that death (i.e., the spirit of death) will not be destroyed until the end of the Millennium. Therefore it is obvious that if the Millennium is to be a time of peace, it will be that way because of the law and order enforced by the members of Christ's government and His army.

Christ will also "rule them with a rod of iron" (Rev. 19:15), indicating that severe discipline will be required. Considering the fact that many people on earth have become accustomed to participating in democratic forms of government, there is likely to be much rebellion against the strict laws that will be imposed by Christ Jesus on those who remain on earth after His judgment of the nations. Thus it is logical that the officials of His government and His army will be required to strictly enforce His laws.

Summary and Concluding Remarks

From the preceding study of Biblical texts it is apparent that the marriage supper of the Lamb will be an outstanding future event which all true Christians should anxiously anticipate. It represents the climax in the lives of those Christians who are invited to attend; it is the time at which the ruling Christians will be united with their Lord and King, Christ Jesus, for all eternity. Following this union they will become ruling members in Christ's everlasting government.

Other than God the Father, Christ Jesus the bridegroom, and His angels, the two primary participating groups in this divine marriage ceremony are the Christians who constitute the bride and the body of Christ. In accordance with God's law concerning marriage, these two groups will be merged into one group and united with their King, Christ Jesus, via the marriage ceremony. Thereafter, this unified group of Christians is referred to as the *"the bride, the Lamb's wife"* (Rev. 21:9).

The first group of Christians, constituting the bride of Christ prior to the wedding ceremony, is a very special group – the Christian martyrs, who gave up their lives in defense of the gospel of Christ Jesus. They are uniquely qualified to be His bride, for they gave up their lives for Him just as He gave His life for them and for others on the cross at Calvary. Since each of these Christians must have died a martyr's death prior to the marriage ceremony, their souls and spirits will be waiting at the altar in heaven when the ceremony begins (see Rev. 6:9-11).

The second group, making up the body of Christ, will be formed from two separate sub-groups:

1. Those qualified Christians who died physically (not as martyrs) prior to the wedding event and whose souls have been residing in Paradise, and

2. Living Christians who will be taken to the wedding site via the rapture of the Christian saints.

Paul addresses these two sub-groups in his description of the rapture in 1 Thess. 4:13-17. At the time of the rapture, all of these participants will receive their imperishable bodies in accordance with Paul's statement in 1 Cor. 15:42-44. Thus they will be prepared for their future roles as rulers in Christ's millennial kingdom.

There is a third group of Christians who will attend the marriage ceremony – Christians who have been called to be servants of God in His heavenly temple. These Christians are expected to attend the divine marriage ceremony as guests of the bridegroom, Christ Jesus. At the conclusion of the marriage ceremony they will be taken to God's temple where they can begin performing their acts of service.

Following the rapture and the divine marriage ceremony, those who have been chosen to be members of Christ's bride and body will become judges and rulers over the inhabitants of the earth. Under Christ, these judges and rulers will control and govern the citizens of earth throughout the Millennium.

I hope that this article will serve to clarify the Biblical teachings concerning the marriage supper of the Lamb and that Christians will be able to anticipate and prepare for this and other events of the future with some degree of certainty. It is my strong conviction that the final seven-year tribulation period is about to begin. Therefore, it is time for all Christians to renew and strengthen their relationships with their Heavenly Father and with Christ Jesus through prayer and fasting.

E. "Berk" Hammond

GOD'S FOUR PROCLAIMED FUTURE JUDGMENTS
(First released in September 2008)

*   *   *   *   *   *   *

Introduction

The Bible contains a great deal of information about the ways in which God will judge the citizens of earth after their physical lives have ended. His future judgments have been the subject of many lectures and sermons in the past, but the conclusions that these teachers and preachers have reached often differ considerably.

These differences are no doubt a result of the fact that their conclusions have sometimes not been approved by the Holy Spirit. When interpreting Bible prophecy, there is little room for human logic, and any conclusions that are not based strictly on the scriptures of the Bible should be clearly identified as such.

In Heb. 9:27 we find this statement: *"And as it is appointed for men to die once, but after this the judgment."* From this verse it is clear that everyone is destined to face some type of spiritual judgment after death, and as we study the scriptures we will find that some may even face more than one of these judgments before they are taken to their final destinations.

The purpose of this article is to examine the Bible texts that relate to God's various judgments and to show them in their proper perspectives. The discussion of these topics will be of primary interest to those who have studied and have an interest in eschatology.

The Four Judgments

The Bible refers to four separate and distinct occasions at which the past works of various segments of humanity will be judged in the future. These events are:

1. The Judgment of the Jews – Ezek. 20:33-38
2. The *"Bema"* Judgment of Christians – 2 Cor. 5:10
3. The Judgment of the Nations – Matt. 25:31-46
4. The Great White Throne Judgment – Rev. 20:11-15

According to John 5:22, God the Father judges no one; He has committed all judgment to Jesus. However, when we examine the first and last judgments listed above it seems that this statement might not apply to the judgment of the Jews – their judgment may be reserved for Jehovah God alone. According to several Old Testament prophets, God considered the nation Israel to be His wife (see Isaiah 54:4-8; Jeremiah 31:32; Ezekiel 16:30-32), and it might not be appropriate for Him to let Jesus, His Son, judge His wife. Therefore we might expect to see Christ Jesus as the presiding Judge at only the second and third judgments listed above, since those to be judged in the first and the last judgments include members of the Jewish race.

All of these judgments are events in which the souls or the bodies of large groups of people will stand before Jehovah God or Christ Jesus in judgment. Now in order to determine the specific nature of these judgments, it will be necessary to explore the pertinent scriptures of the Bible. The four items of specific interest will be: (1) the persons who will be judged, (2) the time of their judgment, (3) the basis on which their judgments will be made, and (4) the sentences to be imposed on the defendants, whether good or bad.

Three other divine judgments or decisions should be mentioned here in addition to those listed above:

1. The judgment of a person's past works at the time of his or her death, leading to a decision as to whether the person's soul should be taken to Paradise or to Hades.

2. The selection of the ruling Christians to be taken in the pre-tribulational partial rapture.

3. The selection of living persons qualified to be taken in the final harvest rapture.

The first of these three divine decisions is exemplified in Jesus' story of Lazarus and the rich man, given in Luke 16:19-31. Next, the selection of Christians to be taken in the partial rapture is described in the Parable of the Ten Virgins in Matt. 25:1-13. The third divine decision listed above will be made simply on the basis of whether the person is or is not a "born-again" Christian. Since none of these three decisions are listed as a "judgment" in the Bible, they will not be included for discussion in this paper.

The Books of Life and Works

Before beginning a discussion of the four divine judgments, it seems appropriate to explore what the Bible has to say about two very important books that will be used in these judgments – the Book of Life and the Books of Works. They are mentioned in connection with the Great White Throne Judgment in Rev. 20:12, which reads as follows: *"And I saw the dead, small and great, standing before God, and books were opened. And another book was opened, which is the Book of Life. And the dead were judged according to their works, by the things which were written in the books."*

This passage mentions two different types of books to be used in the future divine judgment of people – the Book of Life, and the Books of Works. Because these books play a very important role in the divine judgments, it seems appropriate to explore what the Bible has to say about their contents.

The Book of Life

The Book of Life is mentioned several times in both the Old and the New Testaments, but its meaning and significance is largely misunderstood by Christians today. One common but erroneous belief is that it is a book containing only the names of regenerated Christians, and that they were written there at the time of their conversion experiences. Bible scriptures will show these beliefs to be incorrect.

With regard to the names written in the Book of Life, the Bible clearly states that the names of both Christians and Jews will be included. In his letter to the Philippian church, Paul said: *"And I urge you also, true companion, help these women who labored with me in the gospel, with Clement also, and the rest of <u>my fellow workers, whose names are in the Book of Life.</u>"* (Phil. 4:3) This shows that the names of Paul's Christian fellow workers are written in this Book, and it is logical to assume that the names of other Christians will be found there also.

As a part of the prophetic message that was given to Daniel by an angelic messenger, the angel said: *"At that time Michael shall stand up, the great prince who stands watch over the sons of your people; and there shall be a time of trouble, such as never was since there was a nation, even to that time. And at that time <u>your people</u> shall be delivered, <u>every one who is found written in the book.</u>" (Dan. 12:1)* When the angel said "your people," he was obviously referring to Daniel's people, the Jews. Therefore we may conclude that the Book of Life will contain the names of Jews as well as Christians. Furthermore, it will be shown later that God wrote these names into the Book at the time of creation.

One question invariably arises when considering this subject: "Is everyone's name listed in the Book of Life, and if not, why not?" The answer to that question is "No" – everyone's name is not listed in this Book. Those listed in this Book are referred to as God's "elect" persons (see Matt. 24:22, 24, 31), and all others are members of a "non-elect" group. Jesus explained this fact in His parable of the tares in the wheat field – the good seeds represent the "sons of the kingdom" (the elect), and the tares represent the "sons of the evil one" (the non-elect). This parable is given in Matt. 13:24-30; 36-43, and it is given a full interpretation in the companion article entitled "Tares in the Wheat Field."

Jesus emphasized this fact further when He told His disciples: *"<u>Every plant which My heavenly Father has not planted</u> will be uprooted. Let them alone. They are blind leaders of the blind. And if the blind leads the blind, both will fall into a ditch."* (Matt 15:13-14) Unfortunately, there are some on this earth who will never be able to find any type of salvation. Considering this fact, every "one-on-one" evangelist should pray to receive the gift of the discernment of spirits (see 1 Cor. 12:10) so that he or she will not waste time trying to bring a "non-elect" person into the kingdom of God. Of course Satan would like very much to have Jesus' evangelists waste time on his "decoys."

As for the time at which names were written into the Book, this time is specified in Rev. 13:8: *"All who dwell on the earth will worship him [the Antichrist], whose names have not been written in the Book of Life of the Lamb slain from the foundation of the world."* From this it is apparent that if a person's name is written in the Book of Life, it was written there at the time of creation and not at the time of an individual's spiritual regeneration. This is confirmed in Rev. 17:8, so we may conclude that there is nothing a person can do to get his or her name entered into the Book of Life if it was not entered at the time of creation.

With regard to a person's regeneration experience, that is the time at which God the Father draws the person into the kingdom of heaven. In John 6:44 we read: *"No one can come to Me unless the Father who sent Me draws him; and I will raise him up at the last day."* From this we may conclude that a parson's conversion experience is the result of his or her being drawn into the kingdom by God the Father, working through the Holy Spirit, and obviously He will not draw anyone whose name is not written in His Book of Life.

Although a person's name cannot be entered into this Book, apparently it can be erased, if necessary. When Moses was discussing the sins of his people with God on Mt. Sinai he said: *"Oh, these people have committed a great sin, and have made for themselves a god of gold! Yet now, if You will forgive their sin – but if not, I pray, blot me out of Your book which You have written."* The Lord then said to Moses, *"Whoever has sinned against Me, I will blot him out of My book."* (Exod. 32:31-33) Therefore God can and will take a person's name out of His Book of Life if and when it becomes necessary to do so.

Of course, one reason for having potential Christians' names removed from the Book of Life would be their continued refusal to accept their invitations to yield their lives to Christ Jesus. Only God knows how many times a person can refuse His invitation before his or her name is erased from the Book of Life.

The above facts concerning the Book of Life can be summarized briefly as follows:

- The Book of Life was generated and the names of God's elect were written into it at the time of the creation of the world.

- The names that have been entered in the Book are the names of persons who are destined to receive some type of salvation, either Christian salvation for eternal life in the New Jerusalem, or Hebrew salvation for life on the new earth.

- The persons who have their names written in the Book of Life are collectively referred to as God's "elect."

- The Book contains the names of both Christians and Jews, and there are some good reasons to believe that the names of some non-Christian Gentiles may also be included.

- There is no way in which a person whose name is not written in the Book can have his or her name entered into it.

- Although new names cannot be added to the Book, names can be erased when necessary.

The Books of Works

There is not much to be said about the Books of Works other than to say that they contain a listing of all of the works, both good and bad, that have been committed by each person whose name is listed in the Book of Life. There is no reason to list the works of other non-elect persons in these Books, for according to Rev. 20:15 they are automatically doomed to destruction.

In the description of the Books of Works given in Rev. 20:12, the plural form of the word is used, indicating that there will be more than one book to be consulted. Considering the very large number of persons in the "elect" group, and the large number of works that each person performs that are worthy of being recorded, the Books of Works must consist of a very large number of volumes. Of course, it is quite possible that these works (and also the names listed in the Book of Life) may be recorded in the memory banks of a very large computer, but this is only a speculation.

Now that the scriptures relating to these two important types of books have been explored, we can turn our attention back to God's four divine judgments.

The Judgment of the Jews

In the last half of the tribulation period, the Jews will be driven out of their land by the forces of the Antichrist because of their refusal to worship him (see Dan. 9:27; Matt. 24:15-22). Then, according to Rev. 12:13-14, Israel will be driven into the wilderness where God will protect her for 3½ years. These verses read as follows:

> *(13) Now when the dragon [Satan] saw that he had been cast to the earth, he persecuted the woman [Israel] who gave birth to the male Child.*
> *(14) But the woman was given two wings of a great eagle, that she might fly into the wilderness to her place, where she is nourished for a time and times and half a time [3½ years], from the presence of the serpent [Satan].*

This passage (in connection with Dan. 9:27) tells us that Israel will be living in her wilderness hideout during the last 3½ years of the tribulation period. Then, according to Ezek. 20:33-38, God will meet with them in their desert sanctuary and judge them there:

> *(33) As surely as I live, declares the Sovereign LORD, I will rule over you with a mighty hand and an outstretched arm and with outpoured wrath.*
> *(34) I will bring you from the nations and gather you from the countries where you have been scattered – with a mighty hand and an outstretched arm and with outpoured wrath.*
> *(35) I will bring you into the desert of the nations and there, face to face, I will execute judgment upon you.*
> *(36) As I judged your fathers in the desert of the land of Egypt, so I will judge you, declares the Sovereign LORD.*
> *(37) I will take note of you as you pass under my rod, and I will bring you into the bond of the covenant.*

(38) I will purge you of those who revolt and rebel against me. Although I will bring them out of the land where they are living, yet they will not enter the land of Israel. Then you will know that I am the LORD. (NIV)

This passage was taken from the NIV Bible, because it seems to define the judgment in more precise terms. Please note the following items in the above passage:

- It is quite clear that the Judge is Jehovah God, and not Christ Jesus. He will judge all of the Jews that have been driven into the wilderness by the Antichrist.

- These Jews will be judged in the same way that God judged their fathers in the desert outside of the land of Egypt, i.e., their works will be judged.

- The place of judgment is the "desert of the nations," assumed to be their wilderness hideout, into which they have been driven by the Antichrist.

- The purpose of this judgment is apparently to keep the unworthy Jews from reentering the land of Israel after the Antichrist and his false prophet have been thrown into the lake of fire.

The "*Bema*" Judgment of Christians

The future judgment of all Christians was predicted by Paul in 2 Cor. 5:10: *"For we must all appear before the judgment seat of Christ, that each one may receive the things done in the body, according to what he has done, whether good or bad."* The term "judgment seat" used here comes from the Greek word *"bema,"* the word used in the original Greek text. Therefore this judgment is often referred to as the *"Bema"* Judgment.

The *"bema"* judgment seat was used by the Romans to judge and reward athletes and victorious soldiers for their meritorious accomplishments. Therefore, it is understandable why Paul used this word to describe the place where Christians will receive their rewards based on the way in which they have lived their past lives on earth.

The way in which this judgment will be conducted is shown in

Jesus' parable of the talents (Matt. 25:14-30), or the parable of the "minas" (Luke 19:12-27). These parables tell how Jesus will judge and reward Christians for what they have done for Him on earth. They also show how He will punish those who have done nothing for Him. From these two parables it is also apparent that the faithful servants will be rewarded by giving them authority to rule over selected cities under Christ Jesus during the coming Millennium.

In another of my articles titled "Closing Events of the Church Age," I explained that, subsequent to the final harvest rapture, two separate and distinct groups of Christian souls will reside in heaven. These will be the serving Christians mentioned in Rev. 7:15 (the "called" Christians in Matt. 22:14) and the ruling Christians mentioned in Rev. 20:4 (the "chosen" Christians in Matt. 22:14). This earlier document also showed that only the ruling Christians will be taken in the partial rapture prior to the tribulation, and that all true Christians who are left behind will be taken later in the harvest rapture.

Now the faithful servants identified in the parables of the talents and the minas were rewarded by giving them a number of cities over which to rule. This means that these two parables can only relate to the judgment of the ruling Christians, who will be taken from earth via the partial rapture. Serving Christians are not destined to be rulers; consequently these two parables do not apply to them.

In 2 Cor. 5:10, Paul said that <u>all</u> Christians will have to come before the judgment seat of Christ, not just the ruling Christians. Therefore, in order to see how the serving Christians will be judged, it will be necessary to examine other passages of scripture.

First of all, it should be recognized that the *"Bema"* Judgment is strictly a judgment of the works that were accomplished by Christians while they were living on the earth. Then Rev. 19:7-8 states: *"Let us be glad and rejoice and give Him glory, for the marriage of the Lamb has come, and His wife has made herself ready. And <u>to her it was granted to be arrayed in fine linen</u>, clean and bright, for <u>the fine linen is the righteous acts of the saints</u>."*

From this we may conclude that the Christians who constitute the bride of Christ will be clothed in fine linen wedding garments, which will probably be given to them at the time of the final harvest rapture on the basis of their previous righteous acts.

Preparations for this wedding feast are also described in another passage of scripture – the parable of the wedding feast – given in Matt.

22:2-14. Verses 11-13 in this text provide additional information with regard to the wedding garments:

> *(11) But when the king came in to see the guests, he saw a man there who did not have on a wedding garment.*
> *(12) So he said to him, "Friend, how did you come in here without a wedding garment?" And he was speechless.*
> *(13) Then the king said to the servants, "Bind him hand and foot, take him away, and cast him into outer darkness; there will be weeping and gnashing of teeth."*

From this passage it is apparent that <u>all</u> of the wedding guests (including the called Christians) are expected to wear special garments for this special occasion. We may conclude that these special garments will be issued to all Christians worthy to receive them following the harvest rapture. This would then constitute the *"Bema"* Judgment for the "called" Christians.

The Judgment of the Nations

The Judgment of the Nations is a judgment that will be imposed on everyone who is alive on earth at the Second Coming of Christ Jesus, and it is described in Matt. 25:31-46. However, it has been misunderstood by some of our church leaders, for many of them teach that those being judged will include Christians. However, according to the Book of Revelation, there will be no Christians left on earth to be judged at the time of this judgment.

By way of explanation, the Book of Revelation presents us with a listing of the coming eschatological events in their proper chronological order, beginning in Chapter 8. Now the harvest rapture is described in Rev. 14:14-16, and it will be the fulfillment of Jesus' promise given in John 6:38-39. In this passage, Jesus told His disciples: *"For I have come down from heaven, not to do My own will, but the will of Him who sent Me. This is the will of the Father who sent Me, that of <u>all He has given Me I should lose nothing, but should raise it up at the last day</u>."* The "last day" that is mentioned here would of course be the last day of the church, since all true Christians will be taken from earth into heaven at the time of this event.

Then by way of comparison, the Second Coming of Christ Jesus is pictured in Rev. 19:11-21 subsequent to the harvest rapture of the church. Therefore is quite safe to conclude that there will be no true Christians left alive on earth at the time of Jesus' Second Coming. Only non-Christians will be judged in the Judgment of the Nations, excluding the Jews who will have been judged previously by God in the Judgment of the Jews.

In the opening Verses 31-32 of the judgment passage in Matthew 25, we read: *"When the Son of Man comes in His glory, and all the holy angels with Him, then He will sit on the throne of His glory. All the nations will be gathered before Him, and He will separate them one from another, as a shepherd divides his sheep from the goats."*

It is from these verses that the title "Judgment of the Nations" is derived, but this title is somewhat misleading. It seems quite obvious that it will be the individual citizens of the nations that will be judged, probably one nation at a time, and not the nations themselves. Nations, as such, cannot be judged, rewarded and punished in the way that is described in subsequent verses of this scripture passage.

Verses 34-45 of this text describe the basis of this judgment and the manner in which it will be conducted. In short, it will be based on the way in which each individual has treated Jesus – either giving or not giving Him food, water, shelter, clothes, etc. But of course the non-Christian defendants will express their surprise at these judgments, and they will ask when they had ever seen Jesus to give Him any of these things. Then they will be told: *"...inasmuch as you did it to one of the least of these My brethren, you did it to Me."* Likewise, He will say to the "goats, *"...inasmuch as you did not do it to one of the least of these, you did not do it to Me."* (Verses 40 & 45)

Now when Jesus said "these My brethren" He was obviously referring to His Jewish relatives. Therefore, this judgment can be considered to be a fulfillment of the promise that God made to Abram when He said: *"I will bless those who bless you [and your descendants], And I will curse him who curses you [and your descendants]; And in you [and your descendants] all the families of the earth shall be blessed."* (Gen. 12:3) From this it is apparent that the non-Christian Gentiles who are alive on earth when Jesus returns will be judged on the basis of how they have treated the Jews and the nation Israel.

As for their rewards for being kind to the Jews, the righteous "sheep" will be told: *"Come, you blessed of My Father, inherit the kingdom prepared for you from the foundation of the world."* (Verse 34) Of course, the kingdom that was "prepared from the foundation of the world" would have to be the earth itself, for the book of Genesis does not describe the preparation of any other places of residence at the time of creation.

Then in Verse 46 we are told that the unrighteous "goats" will be sent to a place of everlasting punishment – to hell, or the lake of fire. Thus we may conclude that the two purposes of the Judgment of the Nations are: (1) to select those persons who are worthy to remain on earth as citizens of Christ Jesus' kingdom during the Millennium, and (2) to remove all anti-Semitic troublemakers from the earth.

The Great White Throne Judgment

The last of the four judgments, the Great White Throne Judgment, is probably the one that is least understood today. There are some who say that this will not be a judgment at all, but rather an occasion at which all non-Christians left on the earth will be gathered together and thrown into the lake of fire. However, let us now explore the scriptures in order to find the real truth about this judgment.

This judgment will occur at the end of the Millennium, since it is described in Rev. 20:11-15:

> *(11) Then I saw a great white throne and Him who sat on it, from whose face the earth and the heaven fled away. And there was found no place for them.*
> *(12) And I saw the dead, small and great, standing before God, and books were opened. And another book was opened, which is the Book of Life. And the dead were judged according to their works, by the things which were written in the books.*
> *(13) The sea gave up the dead who were in it, and death and Hades delivered up the dead who were in them. And they were judged, each one according to his works.*
> *(14) Then death and Hades were cast into the lake of fire. This is the second death.*
> *(15) And anyone not found written in the Book of Life was cast into the lake of fire.*

From the description of the all-powerful Judge given in Verse 11, it is evident that He must be Jehovah God rather than Christ Jesus. These verses also clearly define the defendants in this judgment. The souls of all non-Christians, including Jews and gentiles, will be taken from their graves, from Hades, or from their living bodies to face Jehovah God in this judgment. This group may include some souls who have been judged previously in either the Judgment of the Jews or the Judgment of the Nations, but this will be a first-time experience for the majority of these souls.

The basis of this judgment is also made clear in these verses. Verses 12-13 state that these souls will be judged on the basis of their past works – works done during their past lives on earth and possibly also in Hades, as they are recorded in the Books of Works in heaven. Their works will be judged to be either righteous or unrighteous, and only Jehovah God will be able to determine which of these two work types is predominant in each case.

One other requirement for being judged righteous is given in Verse 15 – the person's name must be recorded in the Book of Life. However, it is quite obvious that this is not a basis for judgment, but rather a prerequisite for being judged. All persons not having their names recorded in the Book of Life will be automatically thrown into the lake of fire, therefore, there is no need for them to be judged.

As I explained earlier, if a person's name is written in this Book of Life, it was written there when the world was first created. When God created the universe, He wrote the names of everyone destined to have any type of salvation (His "elect") in the Book of Life. Of course this Book would have to include the names of those Christians who will populate the New Jerusalem, and also the Jews and Gentiles who will populate the new earth.

The objective of this judgment is not made clear in the Rev. 20 passage, so other scriptures must be explored to find its purpose. In the next two verses of scripture (Rev. 21:1-2) it is apparent that immediately following this judgment, the old earth and heaven will be replaced by a new earth and a new heaven. Then the next few verses describe the "New Jerusalem," an enormous city that will be the final home for all Christians. It will be mounted on the new earth, supported by twelve foundations, and each foundation will be named for one of the twelve apostles (see Rev. 21:14).

In Rev. 21:12-13, we see that this great city will have twelve gates, each one named for one of the twelve tribes of Israel. Then Rev. 21:24-26 provides some additional information as follows:

> *(24) And the nations of those who are saved shall walk in its light, and the kings of the earth bring their glory and honor into it.*
> *(25) Its gates shall not be shut at all by day (there shall be no night there).*
> *(26) And they shall bring the glory and the honor of the nations into it.*

From these verses it seems obvious that those who are judged to be righteous in the Great White Throne Judgment will populate the new earth, and that they will be citizens of nations, with kings to rule over them. Furthermore, these kings and their subjects will be allowed to visit the New Jerusalem, entering through its twelve gates. The immediate question is: "How did the inhabitants of the new earth come to be there?" It seems fairly obvious that these inhabitants of the new earth must be those who were judged to be righteous in the Great White Throne Judgment just prior to the formation of the new earth.

The salvation that the inhabitants of the new earth will receive will be quite different from that which the Christians will enjoy, in that they will not have the eternal life that will be given to all Christians. Perhaps the best description of life on the new earth can be found in Isaiah 65:17-25 and in Ezekiel, Chapters 40-48. Although the citizens of the new earth will live long lives (see Isaiah 65:22), they will eventually die. This topic is covered in more detail in another of my articles titled "Hebrew Salvation."

From the above discussion it seems clear that the two purposes of the Great White Throne Judgment will be: (1) to select those souls that are worthy to become citizens of the new earth when it is formed, and (2) to remove all non-elect troublemakers. Thus we see that the purposes of this judgment will be quite similar to those of the Judgment of the Nations – i.e., to select those persons qualified to enter into the next phase of God's overall program and to eliminate all troublemakers.

Summary

The coverage, time, basis and purpose of these four divine judgments can be summarized as follows:

The Judgment of the Jews

1. Biblical Text – Ezek. 20:33-38

2. Coverage of the Judgment – Jehovah God will judge all of the Jews that have been driven into their desert hideout by the forces of the Antichrist.

3. Time of the Judgment – This judgment of Israeli citizens will take place at the end of the seven-year tribulation period.

4. Basis of the Judgment – Each Jewish person will be judged on the basis of his or her past works, whether good or bad.

5. Purpose of the Judgment – The purpose of this judgment is to select the Jews who are qualified to return to their native land to live under Christ Jesus as their King during the Millennium.

The *"Bema"* Judgment

1. Biblical Texts – 2 Cor. 5:10; Matt. 25:14-30; Luke 19:12-27

2. Coverage of the Judgment – Christ Jesus will judge all Christians after they have been taken into heaven via the harvest rapture. Christians who have died previously will also be included.

3. Time of the Judgment – This judgment will occur immediately following the harvest rapture.

4. Basis of the Judgment – Each Christian will be judged on the basis of his or her past works, whether good or bad.

5. Purpose of the Judgment – The purpose of this judgment will be to give special rewards or punishment to the Christians being judged.

The Judgment of the Nations

1. Biblical Text – Matt. 25: 31-46

2. Coverage of the Judgment – Christ Jesus will judge each non-Christian person who is alive on earth at the time of His Second Coming, excluding the Jews, who will have been judged previously by Jehovah God in the desert.

3. Time of the Judgment – This judgment will occur at the Second Coming of Christ Jesus, subsequent to the battle of Armageddon.

4. Basis of the Judgment – Each person will be judged on the basis of their previous treatment of the Jews and the nation Israel.

5. Purpose of the Judgment – The purpose of this judgment will be to select the non-Christians who are worthy to remain as citizens of Christ Jesus' kingdom on earth during the coming Millennium and to remove all anti-Semitic troublemakers.

The Great White Throne Judgment

1. Biblical Text – Rev. 20: 11-15

2. Coverage of the Judgment – Jehovah God will judge the soul of every non-Christian person who has his or her name written in the Book of Life. All others will be cast into the lake of fire.

3. Time of the Judgment – This judgment will occur at the end of Christ's millennial rule on the earth, just prior to the replacement of the old heaven and earth with the new heaven and earth.

4. Basis of the Judgment – Each person will be judged on the basis of his or her past works on earth, and possibly in Hades.

5. Purpose of the Judgment – The purpose of this judgment will be to select those Jews and non-Christians who are qualified to live on the new earth when it is formed.

It is my hope that this document will serve to clarify the coverage, the timing, the basis, and the purpose of God's four future divine judgments. It is also my hope and prayer that the Holy Spirit will enable each reader to fully understand God's plan for the future of all mankind and to do his or her part in making everyone ready to face the coming judgments.

E. "Berk" Hammond

THE TIMING OF THE BATTLE OF GOG AND MAGOG

(First released in December 1984)

*   *   *   *   *   *   *

Contents

*   *   *   *   *   *   *

Introduction

The book of Ezekiel predicts a gigantic future battle in which a man referred to as Gog, prince in a land called Magog, will lead his armies into battle against the nation Israel. The name Magog was originally given to a grandson of Noah (see Gen. 10:2), and he and his family settled far north of Jerusalem in the land which is now recognized as southern Russia, or possibly northern Turkey. Therefore, it is generally conceded that a ferocious leader, who will be the ruler of a nation to be located in the land originally occupied by Magog and his family, will some day rise to power and lead a large army in an attack against the nation Israel.

Since this prophecy has not been fulfilled as of this time, we may expect it to be fulfilled in the future, but unfortunately, those who study the prophetic scriptures are divided in their opinions concerning the time at which this battle will take place. The purpose of this exegesis is to attempt to clarify the timing of this great battle by carefully examining all of the pertinent Biblical texts. The selected time period must of course satisfy all of the conditions presented in the prophetic scriptures of the Bible.

Various Biblical scholars have proposed differing time periods for this great battle. However, the majority of these scholars have set the time for this battle either (1) slightly preceding or during the final seven-year tribulation period, or (2) near the end of Christ's future millennial rule on earth. In order to determine the correct time period for this colossal event, it will be necessary to investigate and evaluate all that the Bible has to say about this battle.

Before beginning this study, it seems appropriate to state the primary reason that is often given for believing that the battle of Gog and Magog will take place before or during the coming tribulation period. Although there may be more than one reason for this belief, it is usually justified on the basis of the location of this battle passage in the book of Ezekiel.

The description of this battle is preceded by Ezekiel's description of the "valley of the dry bones" (Ezek. 37:1-28), which describes the regathering of the Israelites as a nation prior to the close of the church age. Then the battle description is followed by a passage (Ezek. 39:17-29) that apparently refers to the battle of Armageddon, the final major event of the seven-year tribulation period.

Therefore, if we assume that the prophetic passages in this section of Ezekiel are listed in chronological order, then the battle of Gog and Magog would have to occur between the re-formation of the nation Israel and the battle of Armageddon, the last event of the tribulation period. However, the following discussion will prove this assumption to be questionable. After all, the Old Testament prophets are noted for the lack of order in their prophetic messages.

Israel's Destiny at the Close of the Church Age

This analysis will begin with an investigation of Biblical scriptures that define the series of events Israel will experience during the tribulation period. Then all of the ways in which the battle of Gog and Magog might be fitted into these events will be examined.

One of Daniel's prophecies relating to the tribulation period is found in Dan. 9:26-27:

> *(26) And after the sixty-two weeks Messiah shall be cut off, but not for Himself; and the people [relatives] of the prince who is to come [the Antichrist] shall destroy the city and the sanctuary. The end of it shall be with a flood [see Rev. 12:15-16], and till the end of the war desolations are determined. (27) Then he [the Antichrist] shall confirm a covenant with many for one [Sabbatical] week; But in the middle of the week he shall bring an end to sacrifice and offering. And on the wing of abominations shall be one who makes desolate, even until the consummation, which is determined, is poured out on the desolate.*

This passage of scripture leads to the following conclusions:

1. The tribulation period will begin when the Antichrist confirms his covenant (or peace treaty) with many nations (including Israel) for one Sabbatical week (seven years).

2. The Antichrist will be a man of Roman origin, since Jerusalem and the sanctuary were destroyed by a Roman army under Titus around 70 A.D., and these are stated to be the Antichrist's "people."

3. In the middle of the seven-year covenant the Antichrist will break this covenant and force the Jews to stop making sacrifices and offerings in their temple. Obviously this will infuriate the Jewish people.

This prophecy can be expanded by reading what Jesus had to say about it in His Olivet Discourse (Matt. 24:15-21). These verses read as follows:

> *(15) Therefore when you see the "abomination of desolation," spoken of by Daniel the prophet, standing in the holy place (whoever reads, let him understand),*
> *(16) then let those who are in Judea flee to the mountains.*
> *(17) Let him who is on the housetop not go down to take anything out of his house.*
> *(18) And let him who is in the field not go back to get his clothes.*
> *(19) But woe to those who are pregnant and to those who are nursing babies in those days!*
> *(20) And pray that your flight may not be in winter or on the Sabbath.*
> *(21) For then there will be great tribulation, such as has not been since the beginning of the world until this time, no, nor ever shall be.*

In these verses Jesus directed the Jews to "flee to the mountains" when the "abomination of desolation" is set up in their temple, and all of the righteous Jews are likely to obey His command. This prophecy is expanded further in Rev. 12:13-17:

> *(13) Now when the dragon [representing Satan] saw that he had been cast to the earth, he persecuted the woman [representing Israel] who gave birth to the male Child.*
> *(14) But the woman was given two wings of a great eagle, that she might fly into the wilderness to her place, where she is nourished for a time and times and half a time, from the presence of the serpent.*
> *(15) So the serpent spewed water out of his mouth like*

*a flood [see Dan. 9:26] after the woman, that he might
cause her to be carried away by the flood.
(16) But the earth helped the woman, and the earth
opened its mouth and swallowed up the flood, which the
dragon had spewed out of his mouth.
(17) And the dragon was enraged with the woman, and
he went to make war with the rest of her offspring, who
keep the commandments of God and have the testimony
of Jesus Christ.*

From this we can conclude the following:

1. Satan will bring intense persecution on the nation Israel
    when his agent, the Antichrist, turns against them in the
    middle of his seven-year covenant.

2. The nation Israel will be taken to a place of safety and
    security in the wilderness during the last 3½ years of the
    tribulation period.

3. After his attempts to persecute the nation Israel fail, he will
    then turn his attention to the persecution of Christians.

The prophet Zechariah completes this scenario by describing what
will happen to Israel at the conclusion of these events. In Zech. 12:10-14,
we are told that Jesus will finally meet with the remnant of the Jewish
nation and pour out on them "the Spirit of grace and supplication."
Then there will be an extensive period of mourning in Israel when they
finally discover the true identity of their Messiah.

What About the Battle of Gog and Magog?

In reviewing the scenario of events predicted for Israel in the scripture
passages listed above, there does not appear to be any way in which the
battle of Gog and Magog can be fitted into this picture. The following
facts are evident as we review these scriptures:

1. The leader, Gog, is not the Antichrist. Gog comes from a
    Russian background, whereas the Antichrist comes from
    a Roman background.

2. The nation Israel will be driven out of their land by the Antichrist and his false prophet, not by Gog and his armies.

3. "Gog and Magog" is not another name for the battle of Armageddon. The people of Israel will not be living in "peace and safety" and in "unwalled villages" when the battle of Armageddon is fought – they will be living in their wilderness hideout.

In summary, there does not seem to be any way to fit the events predicted for the battle of Gog and Magog into Israel's end-time scenario, described in the prophetic Biblical texts listed above.

God's Timing for the Battle of Gog and Magog

Let us turn our attention to the battle of Gog and Magog as described in Ezek. 38:1 through Ezek. 39:16. For the sake of brevity, only those verses of special significance in this passage will be presented here.

In Ezek. 38:8, God gives this message to Gog: "... *In the latter years you [Gog] will come into the land of those brought back from the sword and gathered from many people on the mountains of Israel, ...*" Here God states that Gog will attack Israel "*in the latter years.*" Now this cannot be construed to mean any time near the end of the church age, for there would still be another 1,000 years to follow during the Millennium. Therefore when God said "in the latter years" He meant in the latter years of the Millennium. This conclusion is supported by Rev. 20:7-9:

> *(7) Now when the thousand years [i.e., the years of the Millennium] have expired, Satan will be released from his prison*
>
> *(8) and will go out to deceive the nations which are in the four corners of the earth, Gog and Magog, to gather them together to battle, whose number is as the sand of the sea.*
>
> *(9) They went up on the breadth of the earth and surrounded the camp of the saints [Israel] and the beloved city [Jerusalem]. And fire came down from God out of heaven and devoured them.*

This passage specifically names "Gog and Magog" as a man and a nation that will be in existence at that time, after Satan is released from prison near the end of the Millennium. Furthermore, they will attack the nation Israel. Thus, there should be little room for doubt that the battle of Gog and Magog will take place at that time.

Secondary Considerations

Having explored what the book of Revelation has to say about the battle of Gog and Magog in Chapter 20, consideration will now be given to three other secondary factors that support the conclusions that have been reached thus far.

1. Israel's Safety and Security

Verses 10-11 of Ezekiel Chapter 38 describe the conditions under which Israel will be living when Gog and his armies attack. These verses read as follows:

> *(10) Thus says the Lord God: "On that day it shall come to pass that thoughts will arise in your mind, and you will make an evil plan: You will say,*
> *(11) I will go up against a land of unwalled villages; I will go to a peaceful people, who dwell safely, all of them dwelling without walls, and having neither bars nor gates – "*

These verses indicate that the nation Israel will be living at peace in unwalled villages, without bars or gates at the time they are attacked by Gog and his armies. This is certainly not a good description of the situation in Israel today, where safety and security are in short supply. Even after the Antichrist invokes his seven-year peace treaty with the nation Israel, a considerable amount of time would be required before this peaceful state of existence could be realized. This is another good reason for concluding that this battle of Gog and Magog will not be fought in the immediate future.

Furthermore, after having lived for 1,000 years under the reign of Christ at the end of the Millennium, the nation Israel will definitely be living in peace and safety. At that time they will have no need for walls around their villages or for bars and gates. The living conditions described in Ezekiel Chapter 38 would be quite appropriate for that time period.

2. Gog's Weapons of Warfare

Gog's army, as it is described in Ezek. 38:4,15 and in Ezek. 39:9, would seem to consist primarily of cavalry troops, fighting with swords, bows and arrows, javelins and spears. The use of such primitive weapons is further emphasized in Ezek. 39:9-10 by the fact that these weapons will be combustible and will be burned as fuel in the cities of Israel for seven years. This does not seem to be a good description of the weapons used by the armies of our nations today (tanks, rockets, aircraft, etc.), and this is still another reason to conclude that the battle described in Ezekiel 38 and 39 will not take place in the near future.

Now consider the fact that at the end of the Millennium, all the nations of the world will have been living at peace under the reign of Christ and His saints during the Millennium. Having lived under those conditions for 1,000 years, it is quite apparent that all of their modern weapons of warfare will have been completely destroyed. Consequently, the rebellious citizens of Magog will have to quickly improvise simple weapons to fight the war that is to be waged at that time against Israel under the prompting of Satan.

According to Ezekiel's prophecy, their weapons will be swords, bows and arrows, javelins and spears, some of which will be made of combustible material that can be used for fuel. For transportation, they will have to use a readily available animal – the horse. Thus, at the end of the Millennium, the prophetic predictions given by Ezekiel become much more reasonable.

3. God's Weapons of Destruction

As for the type of destruction to be used by God in destroying Gog and his armies, Rev. 20:9 states that they will be destroyed by fire from heaven. This is in general agreement with Ezek. 38:22 and 39:6, both of which indicate that fire from heaven will be one of the primary weapons to be utilized for the destruction of Gog's armies. This is a third reason to conclude that the wars described in Rev. 20 and in Ezek. 38 and 39 are one and the same.

Summary and Conclusions

The facts listed above all support the hypothesis that the predicted battle of Gog and Magog will be a post-Millennial event. There seems to be no way in which the pertinent Bible prophecies can be legitimately interpreted otherwise. Furthermore, it is quite likely that at the end of the Millennium there will actually be a nation called "Magog," ruled over by a prince having the name of "Gog."

As for the events described in Ezek. 37-48, they are all sequential. However, it must be recognized that there is a 1,000-year gap between Chapters 37 and 38 – the 1,000 years of the Millennium. Then there is another battle described in Ezek. 39:17-29 which must be some battle other than Gog and Magog, since it has already been described fully at this point. This second battle description resembles the description of the battle of Armageddon given in Rev. 19:17-18, and it is probably a flash-back to that battle so that the battles of Gog and Magog and Armageddon can be compared.

There are similarities to be noted as follows when the battles of Armageddon and Gog and Magog are considered. Among them:

1. Satan will instigate both of these battles. In the battle of Armageddon, he will lead the opposing forces through the Antichrist, and in the battle of Gog and Magog he will work through Gog, the prince of Magog.

2. Each of these battles will occur at the end of a major dispensation period. Armageddon will be the concluding event for the church age, and the battle of Gog and Magog will occur at the end of the Millennium.

3. In both battles, God will use supernatural weapons to defeat His enemies – thunder, lightning, a tremendous earthquake, gigantic hailstones, fire and brimstone from heaven, etc.

These facts all seem to indicate that in each of these two battles, God will be subjecting the living citizens of earth to a final examination before a new age begins. He will test them to see if they will choose to be obedient to Him, or if they can be deceived and swayed by a rebellious leader. Only those who have remained faithful to God prior to these battles will be able to reject the temptation to follow Satan's chosen leader into battle. Let us hope that the majority of those who are left on earth at that time will have the wisdom to make the right decision.

The conclusions that have been reached in this document should not be construed to mean that Russia will not try to attack Israel in the near future. They may or may not start a war with Israel. However, such a war should not be identified as the battle of Gog and Magog, described in Ezekiel 38-39, for the outcome will not be in accordance with this passage of scripture. The Antichrist, and not Gog, will be the next major actor in the affairs of the Middle East.

E. "Berk" Hammond

HOW WILL THE MIDDLE EAST WAR END?
(First released in August 2006)

* * * * * * *

The current war in the Middle East between Israel, Hezbollah, Hamas, Lebanon, Syria, and Iran appears to be increasing in intensity, with no apparent end in sight. To make this situation even worse, the leaders in Iran have announced their intention to use nuclear weapons to completely destroy the nation Israel. However, the prophetic scriptures in the Bible predict that this will never happen because Israel will be on hand to welcome the Lord Jesus when He returns to earth (see Zech. 12:9-14). Therefore, we may conclude that the present war will end before Iran's threats materialize. But how will this happen?

There are some who think that God will intervene supernaturally and bring an end to this war. This might be so, but let us first examine the pertinent prophetic scriptures to see what they have to say about the conclusion of this war.

In 2 Thess. 2:1-4, Paul states that Christ's return to earth to establish His Millennial Kingdom will be preceded by the revelation of the "man of sin" – the Antichrist. Then the text of Dan. 9:26-27 provides some useful information concerning his first actions after he is revealed:

(26) And after the sixty-two weeks Messiah shall be cut off, but not for Himself; And the people of the prince who is to come Shall destroy the city and the sanctuary. The end of it shall be with a flood, And till the end of the war desolations are determined.

(27) Then he shall confirm a covenant with many for one week; But in the middle of the week He shall bring an end to sacrifice and offering. And on the wing of abominations shall be one who makes desolate, Even until the consummation, which is determined, Is poured out on the desolate.

These two scripture verses contain a great deal of information about events near the close of the church age, but the item of primary importance in our study is contained in Verse 27. Here we find that the *"prince who is to come"* (the Antichrist) will *"make a firm covenant with the many for one week,"* i.e., for a sabbatical week of seven years. But what does the term *"the many"* mean in this statement?

Note also that in the middle of this seven-year time period the Antichrist will put a stop to the sacrificing of grain offerings that had been prescribed by God for the Jews. Therefore, it seems reasonable to conclude that the Antichrist's covenant will be a peace treaty between Israel and her neighboring Islamic nations. If this is so, then the current Middle East war will be brought to an end by the Antichrist when he arrives on earth from the "bottomless pit."

It is my opinion that the Antichrist will be revealed quite soon and that he will command all of the nations of the Middle East to stop fighting. In Psalm 122:6, we are told to pray for the peace of Jerusalem, but don't be surprised to see their immediate peace ushered in by the Antichrist. In Dan. 9:27 we find that this time of peace will only last for 3½ years. Their lasting peace will not begin until the Second Coming of Christ Jesus at the end of the tribulation period.

E. "Berk" Hammond

RECOGNIZING THE ANTICHRIST

(First released in May 2001)

* * * * * * *

Contents

- Introduction
- Biblical Names for the Antichrist
- The False Satanic Trinity
- From Whence Will Come the Antichrist?
- The Identity of the Antichrist
- Summary and Conclusions

* * * * * * *

Introduction

Most Christians today are aware of at least a few of the Biblical prophecies that relate to the Antichrist – the powerful leader who is expected to dominate all the nations of the world at the close of the church age. Yet there does not appear to be a uniform opinion within the Christian church as to the nature of this individual and the place from which he will come. The purpose of this paper is to explore the passages of scripture that contain information about the Antichrist so that his true nature and his origin can be better defined.

The name "Antichrist" can be found in the Bible only five times, and all of these are in the first two Epistles of John. John introduces this subject in 1 John 2:18-19, 22 as follows:

> *(18) Little children, it is the last hour; and as you have heard that the Antichrist is coming, even now many antichrists have come; by which we know that it is the last hour.*
>
> *(19) They went out from us, but they were not of us; for if they had been of us, they would have continued with us; but they went out that they might be made manifest, that none of them were with us.*
>
> ---
>
> *(22) Who is a liar but he who denies that Jesus is the Christ? He is antichrist who denies the Father and the Son.*

Then John returns to this subject again in 2 John 1:7, which reads as follows: *"For many deceivers have gone out into the world who do not confess Jesus Christ as coming in the flesh. This is a deceiver and an antichrist."* From these verses it is apparent that John makes a distinction between "the Antichrist," and "an antichrist, of which there have been many. The final Antichrist will be the last one of a series, and he will be the subject of this study.

John provides the following additional information in 1 John 4:2-3:

> *(2) By this you know the Spirit of God: "Every spirit that confesses that Jesus Christ has come in the flesh is of God,*
>
> *(3) and every spirit that does not confess that Jesus Christ has come in the flesh is not of God." And this is the spirit of the Antichrist, which you have heard was coming, and is now already in the world.*

These verses introduce the demonic "spirit of the Antichrist." When anyone is possessed or controlled by the spirit of the Antichrist, then that person can be considered to be "an antichrist." However, it will be shown later that "the Antichrist" (the final antichrist of the church age) will be possessed, controlled and empowered by Satan himself, the chief of all antichrist spirits. Satan will provide the supernatural power with which the final Antichrist is to be endowed.

Biblical Names for the Antichrist

Several of the Bible prophets have made reference to the Antichrist, but other than the apostle John, none have called him by that name. Instead, they have used names that either symbolize or describe his nature and character. Some of the names that have been used for the Antichrist are: the "Assyrian," the "Man of Sin," the "Son of Perdition," the symbolic "Beast having seven heads and ten horns" in the Revelation, etc.

Although the names listed above are useful in assessing the nature and character of the Antichrist, the name "Antichrist" is the name by which he is recognized by most Christians. It should be understood that this name is composed of two separate parts – the prefix "Anti" coupled with the familiar titular name "Christ." According to the dictionary this prefix "Anti" can be interpreted to mean "against," or "in place of," and of course the Antichrist will actively oppose the teachings of Jesus and also try to replace Him as the object of worship. Paul addresses this subject in 2 Thess. 2:3-4, which reads as follows:

> *(3) Let no one deceive you by any means; for that Day will not come unless the falling away comes first, and the man of sin is revealed, the son of perdition,*
> *(4) who opposes and exalts himself above all that is called God or that is worshiped, so that he sits as God in the temple of God, showing himself that he is God.*

Thus it is apparent that the Antichrist will deny the basic tenets of the Christian faith and try to replace God as an object of worship.

The False Satanic Trinity

In denying these Christian doctrines, Satan will simply try to replace God, Christ Jesus, and the Holy Spirit with his own false trinity. From the above scripture passage it is apparent that the Antichrist will eventually claim that he is God, and that there is no God to be worshipped other than himself. Thus he will assume the first position in his false trinity. He will try to support this claim based on the many supernatural miracles that he will perform using Satan's spiritual power (see Rev. 13:7).

The above passage from 2 Thessalonians also makes it clear that Christ will not return to earth again until the Antichrist has been seen and recognized. Therefore we can not expect to see Christ, in either the harvest rapture or the Second Coming, before we see the Antichrist.

The second "beast," introduced in Rev. 13:11-18, will fill the second position in the false trinity, and he is identified as the "false prophet" in Rev. 19:20. From these verses it is apparent that the purpose of this second beast is to direct the people's attention to the Antichrist as their primary object of worship, just as Jesus told His followers to worship God the Father. He will perform many miracles, and he will command that an image of the Antichrist be made. He will even cause this image to speak on behalf of the Antichrist, using Satan's supernatural power.

It is my conviction that this image of the Antichrist is what was called the "abomination that causes desolation" by the prophet Daniel and by Jesus (see Dan. 11:31; 12:11; Matt. 24:15 – NIV). As its name implies, this abomination will cause Jerusalem to become desolate because most Jews will refuse to worship this image and will be forced to flee from their land to escape persecution and death (see Rev. 12:13-16). In this latter passage the "woman" who is driven out into the wilderness symbolizes the nation Israel.

Satan himself will fill the third position of the false trinity, and he will provide the spiritual power necessary for the Antichrist and his false prophet to work their many miracles. The way in which the three persons of the false trinity relate to the divine Persons of the Holy Trinity is shown in the following table.

The Holy Trinity	The False Trinity
God the Father	The Antichrist
Christ Jesus the Son	The False Prophet
The Holy Spirit	Satan

The functional relationship between each of the three members of these two trinities is the same in each case. God the Father and the Antichrist are responsible for planning any actions to be taken. Christ Jesus and the False Prophet are responsible for executing the planned actions and leading people to worship their respective leaders. Finally, the Holy Spirit and Satan provide the spiritual power necessary to accomplish supernatural actions. The Antichrist will try to make the False Trinity replace the Holy Trinity throughout his apostate church, which is symbolized by the harlot "Babylon" in Revelation 17.

From Whence Will Come The Antichrist?

This is a topic about which there is much confusion in the body of Christ today, although the Bible provides a very clear answer to this question. For example, most Christians know that the number for the Antichrist, as given in Rev. 13:18 is "666," and that this number can be obtained by assigning numerical values to each letter of his name in accordance with some systematic code.

Various candidates have been proposed on this basis, such as Henry Kissinger, Adolph Hitler, etc. However, this current group of candidates for which the "666" code has been applied have had their names written in modern languages when calculating this number – languages that would have had no meaning or significance in the time that the book of Revelation was written. Therefore, these results are questionable, to say the least.

There is a passage of scripture in Dan. 9:26 which discloses the true origin of the Antichrist. This verse reads: *"And after the sixty-two weeks Messiah shall be cut off, but not for Himself; and <u>the people of the prince who is to come</u> shall destroy the city and the sanctuary. The end of it shall be with a flood, and till the end of the war desolations are determined."* Here it is predicted that the "people of the prince who is to come" will destroy the city (Jerusalem) and the sanctuary. Of course Jerusalem was completely destroyed in 70 AD by the Roman army under the command of Titus; therefore it seems obvious that the Antichrist will be a Roman citizen.

It should be recognized that the two languages in which the New Testament was written (Greek and Aramaic) are both languages in which each letter of the alphabet has an assigned numerical value, to be used in writing numbers. In Greek, the word *"alpha"* had the value of one, *"beta"* had the value of two, *"gamma"* the value of three, etc. Similarly, the letters of the Aramaic alphabet have assigned values to be used for the same purpose. It seems quite likely that in searching for a name that has the numerical value of "666," one of these two languages should be used for writing the candidate's name and calculating his number.

Although the process of calculating the Antichrist's number is understood by most Christians, very few understand what the Bible has to say about the place from which he will come. There are two passages of scripture in the Revelation to John that state precisely the place from which he will come. The first of these is Rev. 17:8, which reads as follows: *"The beast that you saw [symbolizing the Antichrist] was, and is not, and will ascend out of the bottomless pit and go to perdition. And those who dwell on the earth will marvel, whose names are not written in the Book of Life from the foundation of the world, when they see the beast that was, and is not, and yet is."* This scripture is supported by Rev. 11:7, which reads: *"When they [God's two powerful witnesses] finish their testimony, the beast that ascends out of the bottomless pit [the Antichrist] will make war against them, overcome them, and kill them."*

From these two verses of scripture it is apparent that that the Antichrist is a man who: (1) lived at some time before John received his vision on the Isle of Patmos, (2) was dead at the time that John received his vision, and (3) will be resurrected and returned to earth from the "bottomless pit." Then after ruling over the nations of the earth for seven years he will go to his destruction in the lake of fire.

The term "bottomless pit" might be considered to be equivalent to Hades, but it more likely refers to the "great chasm" mentioned by Jesus in His story about the rich man and Lazarus in Luke 16:26. In any case, the fact that the Antichrist will come to us from the bottomless pit means that he will be resurrected from the dead and will therefore have the status of a fallen angel. Since he will try to impersonate Christ Jesus, then he should arrive in the same way that Jesus said that He would arrive – with a host of angels (see Matt. 25:31).

The Antichrist will not be born on the earth a second time; it is quite likely that he will appear as a full-grown visitor from outer space, probably arriving in a space vehicle (commonly called a "UFO"), claiming to be the Jewish Messiah and Christ Jesus returning from heaven to rule over the nations of the world. One reliable way to eliminate any person from a list of tentative Antichrist candidates might be to prove that he was born recently on the earth.

As for the time of his appearance, it is generally believed that the sabbatical week referred to in Dan. 9:27 is the final seven-year period of tribulation at the close of the church age. If this is so, then according to this verse the "prince who is to come" (the Antichrist) will negotiate a seven-year peace treaty with the "many" (the many nations of the Middle East) prior to the beginning of the tribulation period.

Of course, when the Antichrist arrives on earth he will try to make all Christians believe that he is the real Christ, returning to earth to rule over it just as He promised. Consequently, he will undoubtedly come to earth from outer space, just as Matt. 25:31 and Acts 1:10-11 imply that He will. In Matt. 25:31 we are told that He will be accompanied by many of His holy angels, therefore it is likely that when the Antichrist arrives in his space vehicle he will also be accompanied by many of Satan's fallen angels, also riding in space vehicles. This group of fallen angels will probably constitute his army, which will be used to dominate the nations of the earth. This explains the statement which is to be made by the people of the world, *"Who is like unto the beast? Who is able to make war with him?"* (see Rev. 13:4)

Perhaps the first major project that the Antichrist will undertake will be the rebuilding of the Jewish temple, so that he will have a place for the Jews and others to worship him during the last half of his seven-year peace covenant – the time known as the "great tribulation period." In Zech. 6:12-13 we read:

> *(12) Then speak to him, saying, "Thus says the Lord of hosts, saying: 'Behold, the Man [Christ Jesus] whose name is the BRANCH! From His place He shall branch out, and He shall build the temple of the Lord;*
> *(13) Yes, He shall build the temple of the Lord. He shall bear the glory, And shall sit and rule on His throne; so He*

*shall be a priest on His throne, and the counsel of peace
shall be between them both.'"*

Although this passage actually relates to the cleansing (or rebuilding)
of the temple after Christ's Second Coming (as predicted in Dan. 8:13-
14, 26), the Antichrist will probably use it to justify his building the
temple when he arrives on earth.

The Identity of the Antichrist

There have been many persons suggested as candidates for the coming
Antichrist, but most of them fail to meet the conditions outlined in a
previous section of this document. However, there was a book entitled
"Soon-Coming World-Shaking Events," published by the Christian
Missionary Society of Phoenix, Arizona, which contained perhaps the
most plausible suggestion concerning the identity of the Antichrist. This
book asserted that the Antichrist will be the former Emperor of Rome,
Nero Caesar. Nero certainly fulfills the first two conditions of Rev. 17:8
in that he lived on earth before John received his revelation from God,
and he was dead at the time that this revelation was received.

Two additional reasons for selecting Nero Caesar as the primary
candidate for the Antichrist are that: (1) he is a Roman citizen, and (2)
the sum of the numbers assigned to the Aramaic letters that are used
to spell his name is "666," although I have no way of validating this
claim.

God's possible selection of Nero Caesar to be the final Antichrist
appears to be reasonable, since he has had a considerable amount of
experience in persecuting and tormenting Christians and Jews during
his first life on earth. Therefore Nero Caesar seems to have the qualities
necessary to fill this role as a persecutor of God's saints.

Of course any knowledge that we may have concerning the true
identity of the Antichrist will be of little use because it is doubtful
that on the day of his first appearance he will introduce himself by
his former name. Instead, he will probably claim to be the Jewish
Messiah, Christ Jesus, returning to bring peace and healing to our
troubled world. It is expected that he will continue in this initial role
as a kind and benevolent world leader during the first 3½ years of the
tribulation. period

Then, according to Dan. 9:27, he will show his true colors in the middle of this period by ordering the Jews to stop making sacrifices and grain offerings in their temple, and according to Rev. 13:14-15 everyone will be commanded to worship him and his image (probably a statue). As was explained earlier, this image is considered to be the "abomination that brings desolation," which is introduced in Dan. 11:31 and in Dan. 12:11, and is mentioned by Jesus in Matt. 24:15.

Summary and Conclusions

The results of this study can be summarized briefly as follows:

1. There have been many antichrists on earth since the Christian church was first formed – any person who is dominated or controlled by the demonic spirit of antichrist can be labeled an antichrist.

2. The final Antichrist will be different from his predecessors in that he will be dominated and controlled by Satan himself. He will utilize the full spiritual power of Satan, and he will therefore be able to work amazing miracles.

3. The name "antichrist" can be found only in the Biblical Epistles of John. However, several other names are used to describe this person by the writers of other books of the Bible, such as the "Assyrian," the "Man of Sin," the "Son of Perdition," the symbolic "Beast having seven heads and ten horns" in the Revelation, etc.

4. Both the arrival of the Antichrist and the predicted apostasy within the church will precede the rapture of Christians and the Second Coming of Christ.

5. The Antichrist will be one of three members of a False Trinity when he appears, the other members being his false prophet and Satan himself. This False Trinity will duplicate and replace the Holy Trinity within his apostate church.

6. The final Antichrist lived on earth as a Roman citizen prior to the time that John received his revelation from God on the Isle of Patmos. He was dead at the time of

John's revelation, and he will be resurrected and returned to earth from the "bottomless pit" near the beginning of the final tribulation period.

7. The number of the Antichrist, as stated in Rev. 13:18, is "666." This number is obtained by adding together the numerical values assigned to the letters of his name, using a language in which the letters have pre-assigned numerical values, such as Hebrew, Aramaic, Greek or Latin. Considering the conditions outlined in Item 6 above, the best candidate for the Antichrist is probably Nero Caesar, since his number allegedly has been calculated to be "666" when his name is written in Aramaic.

In conclusion, let me say that I have no desire to encounter the Antichrist, but since we know from Biblical prophecy that he must appear on earth before our beloved Savior Christ Jesus can return, then I look forward to his appearance with some fear and trepidation. I pray that all Christians will recognize him for who he is when he does appear, and that they will not be deceived by his false propaganda and his rhetoric.

E. "Berk" Hammond

HEBREW SALVATION
(First released in August 2007)

*   *   *   *   *   *   *

The majority of Christians today focus their attention primarily on those Bible passages that provide instructions for living a good Christian life on earth, and on those that describe future prophetic events leading to their salvation and their promised life in heaven. Of course this is natural, since the primary concern of each Christian should be the eventual destiny of his or her soul and the souls of other Christians. However, Christians are told to love everyone, so it seems that they should also read and understand those Bible passages that relate to the destiny of people outside the Christian faith and be concerned about them, especially their Jewish brethren.

The Bible has much to say about the destiny of the Jews, but unfortunately these messages are largely misunderstood by Christians today. One common belief is that anyone who does not become a "born-again" Christian is automatically doomed to spend eternity in the lake of fire. However, when properly understood, the Bible does not support this belief.

In considering the book of the Revelation to John, we should remember that this book was written primarily for Christians, telling them the events they can anticipate at the close of the church age. Therefore we should not expect to find much information concerning the destiny of non-Christians in this particular book of the Bible.

However, it does provide clues as to where this information can be found in other prophetic books of the Bible.

In 2 Peter 3:10 we are told: *"But the day of the Lord will come as a thief in the night, in which the heavens will pass away with a great noise, and the elements will melt with fervent heat; both the earth and the works that are in it will be burned up."* The time at which this destruction of the earth is to occur must be subsequent to the end of Christ's millennial rule on the earth; obviously, it could not happen before that time. Furthermore, in 2 Peter 3:13 we are told to look for new heavens and a new earth after the old heavens and the old earth have been destroyed.

Then in Rev. 21:1, John the Revelator says: *"Now I saw a new heaven and a new earth, for the first heaven and the first earth had passed away. Also there was no more sea."* The remainder of Chapter 21 is devoted primarily to a description of the new heaven – a tremendously large city called the "New Jerusalem" – the eventual home for God, Christ, and all Christians.

It is significant that this tremendous city will have twelve gates, each one named for one of the tribes of Israel. It will also be supported by twelve foundations, each one named for one of the Christian apostles (see Rev. 21:12-14). These foundations must by definition be the means of support for the city, each one resting on the new earth. Furthermore, the inhabitants of the new earth will use the twelve gates when they wish to visit the large city above them – the New Jerusalem. It is interesting that according to Rev. 21:24-26, the "kings of earth" will bring their glory into the city when they enter it through these gates.

Many Christians focus their attention on the New Jerusalem, their eventual home, and they pay little attention to the purpose for which the new earth will be created, or to the activities that will take place on it. The first and most predominant questions to be raised are: "Who will inhabit the new earth and how will they get to their new home?"

A partial answer to the first of these questions is found in the terms of the covenant that God made with Abraham. One of the terms of this covenant is defined in Gen. 17:7-8 as follows:

> *(7) And I will establish My covenant between Me and you and your descendants after you in their generations, for an everlasting covenant, to be God to you and your descendants after you.*

(8) Also I give to you and your descendants after you the land in which you are a stranger, all the land of Canaan, for <u>an everlasting possession</u>; and I will be their God.

The word "everlasting" used here means "eternal," therefore we should expect to see at least the righteous Jews living on the new earth after it is formed. This supposition is supported by the last two chapters of Ezekiel, which show how the land on the new earth directly under the New Jerusalem will be divided between the twelve tribes of Israel.

Now that it has been determined that the new earth will be populated by at least the righteous Jews, let us investigate the process by which they will be placed there. In Rev. 20:11-15 we find a description of the final judgment of the souls of all dead persons at the end of the Millennium – God's "White Throne Judgment." Of course this will not be a judgment of Christian souls, for they will have been judged much earlier following the final rapture of the church (see 2 Cor. 5:10), and they will be living in their heavenly homes prior to the close of the Millennium.

Verses 12-13 of Rev. 20 make it clear that <u>the souls of all dead persons</u> will be brought before the white throne of God for the final judgment of their works. Of course this would include righteous as well as unrighteous souls, and the purpose of this judgment will be to separate these two groups. Since this judgment will take place just before the creation of the new heavens and the new earth, it seems logical that those persons found to be righteous will be resurrected, given new physical bodies, and placed on the new earth – their new home. For lack of a better name I have called this supernatural action "Hebrew Salvation," in contrast to "Christian Salvation."

It may be difficult for some to believe that the souls of the residents of Hades (or hell, according to the KJV) will be brought out for final judgment before God's white throne, but according to Rev. 20:13, that will happen. Thus Hades can be considered to be only a temporary residence for the non-Christian dead. It is my understanding that the Catholics call this place "Purgatory."

Then from 1 Peter 3:19-20 it is apparent that, during the three days following His death on the cross, Jesus went into Hades and preached to the unrighteous souls who were residing there. If all of these souls were doomed to go automatically into the lake of fire, then

His preaching would have been in vain. It is likely that He told them about their coming final judgment before God's white throne, and it is likely that He encouraged them to show kindness and concern for their fellow prisoners in Hades in order to have some righteous works to their credit prior to their final judgment.

The next question might be: "Will the inhabitants of the new earth include only members of the Jewish faith, or will some righteous Gentiles also be included? According to Rom. 2:14-16, God's judgment of the Gentiles will be based on the extent to which they have followed the dictates of their consciences – those who have been obedient to their consciences might be judged to be righteous and worthy of Hebrew Salvation. This conclusion is supported by the text of Ezek. 47:22-23, which reads:

> *(22) It shall be that you will divide it [the land] by lots as an inheritance for yourselves, and for the <u>strangers who dwell among you and who bear children among you</u>. They shall be to you as native-born among the children of Israel; they shall have an inheritance with you among the tribes of Israel.*
>
> *(23) And it shall be that <u>in whatever tribe the stranger dwells</u>, there you shall give him his inheritance, says the Lord GOD.*

The strangers mentioned in these verses must be Gentiles who have been judged righteous, and who have been resurrected for life on the new earth.

The concluding verse of the white throne judgment, Rev. 20:15, reads: *"And anyone not found written in the Book of Life was cast into the lake of fire."* Many Christian pastors and teachers believe that a person's name is written in the book of life only when he or she experiences spiritual rebirth as a Christian. If this were true, and no Christians are to be judged in the white throne judgment, then everyone who faces God in this judgment would be doomed to destruction.

However, according to Rev. 17:8 this belief is shown to be incorrect. This verse reads: *"The beast that you saw was, and is not, and will ascend out of the bottomless pit and go to perdition. And those who dwell on the earth will marvel, <u>whose names are not written in the Book of Life from</u>*

the foundation of the world, when they see the beast that was, and is not, and yet is." Thus if a person's name is written in the Book of Life, it was written there at the time of creation, and there will be many Jews and Gentiles who have their names in this book without being Christians.

Another question that might be raised is: "What will life on the new earth be like?" Perhaps the best description of the life to be expected on the new earth is to be found in Isaiah 65:17-25 and in Ezekiel Chapters 40-48. It is significant to note that Isaiah states that those living on the new earth will eventually die, but that they will live to be as old as trees (see Verse 22), as did the patriarchs of the Old Testament. Therefore it is apparent that eternal life will not be given to those souls receiving Hebrew Salvation, as it will be given to those receiving Christian Salvation.

As for the tremendous temple that is described in Ezekiel 40-42, it will be the place of worship for the Jews living on the new earth, and according to Zech. 6:12-13 this temple will be built by the Lord Himself. Then in Ezekiel 43 there is given an account of how the Lord will enter this temple and make it His eternal home, allowing Him to live with His adopted people.

It seems that the primary conclusion that Christians might draw from the foregoing discussion is that since Jesus considered it important to preach to the residents of Hades following His death on the cross, it follows that Christians should be concerned and have compassion for them also. It seems appropriate to pray for God to send ministering angels to continue preaching to the inhabitants of Hades, following Jesus' example.

Because the previous discussion had nothing to do with Christian Salvation, this article may be of only passing interest for most Christians. However, I trust that it will shed some light on the destiny of those souls who die outside of the Christian faith. May God richly bless everyone who reads it and becomes prayerfully concerned about the destiny of the Jews, the non-Christian residents of earth, and the residents of Hades.

E. "Berk" Hammond